EMBARRASSED BY THE LIGHT

—By—

Douglas Beardall

Embarrassed By The Light

—by—

Douglas Beardall

LDS BOOK PUBLICATIONS

P.O. Box 1515
Provo, UT 84603-1515

Toll Free 1-800-950-0040   Local 1-801-226-3539
In Utah 1-800-974-4341   Fax 801-221-1177

Other book
Publications by
Douglas Beardall—

For Missionaries Only!
The Qualities of Love
Death and the LDS Family
Mormon Money Matters
The Miracle of Love
Passage to Light
Cookbook for All Seasons
About the Three Nephites
The Missionary Kit
All About Angels - Vol. I
All About Angels - Vol. II
Latter-day Bondage

Typesetting by Myrna Varga
The Office Connection
Provo, Utah

Copyright © 1995 by C. Douglas Beardall
Published by LDS Book Publications, Inc.
Box 1515, Provo, Utah 84603

Printed in the United States of America
ISBN: 1-882371-02-X

—CONTENTS—

Introduction

As we were going to press with this new publication, a good friend of mine asked me why I decided to write an 'expose' about Betty Eadie and her book *Embraced by the Light*. I told him that my first exposure to the "Embraced" book and to Betty Eadie was when a local newspaper began to run advertisements for the lectures Betty was scheduling in towns throughout the state of Utah. The advertisements were actual paragraphs lifted from the book which quoted Betty telling about her alleged journey into the hereafter and her embrace with the Savior. It sounded so untrue and incredible that I dismissed it as just another heretic who was sensationalizing a wishful fantasy for profit, national exposure and her "15 minutes of fame."

Shortly after reading the newspaper ads, a relative, (who serves in a stake calling and is well versed in gospel subjects), gave us the *Embraced by the Light* book as a gift. She very highly recommended the book and told us that we needed to read it as soon as possible. The more I read the book the more distraught I became. It just didn't feel right; and there were many scriptural contradictions throughout the book. As I read it I began to make brief notes in the margins and at the top and bottom of the pages. When something didn't ring true . . . I'd mark it in order to come back and research it later.

The following week, as I was teaching the Gospel Doctrine class in my ward, I asked three questions to the sixty-five adult members of the Mormon Church attending the class. First, I asked, "How many of you <u>have</u> the book entitled

Embraced by the Light by Betty Eadie?" About fifty-five of the sixty-five class members raised their hands. The next question was, "How many of you have **read** the 'Embraced' book?" The same fifty-five students raised their hands. The third question was the one that startled me the most: "How many of you **believe** what Betty Eadie wrote in the book?" I was certain that none of the Mormon readers would raise their hands . . . but was I ever wrong. The same group that purchased the book, and read it, also believed it! Realizing that I was outnumbered, I returned to the safety of the Sunday School manual and finished the assigned lesson. I remained in disbelief and was sorry that I had strayed from the lesson to conduct a "straw poll" after discovering the findings.

I had pretty well forgotten about even finishing the last few chapters in *Embraced by the Light* and had put it away for almost a year, until the strangest thing happened. The afternoon television talk show star, Oprah Winfrey began promoting an upcoming segment about near-death experiences, and Oprah's sole studio guest was to be Betty Eadie. On the allotted day and time, I set my VCR to record the program and when I was able to see the interview, I was dumbfounded. I could not believe my ears . . . or my eyes. Betty Eadie had some colorful, visual computer graphics which coincided with the questions Oprah was asking . . . psychedelic montages which looked like the lead-in to a Star Wars movie and scenes of flowers and waterfalls and stars in the universe.

Admittedly, it was entertaining. However, what made me so indignant and furious was when Betty Eadie stated two separate times, in very plain and direct language, that: "Jesus Christ told me (Betty) that it didn't matter what church a person belonged to, that as long as you have love, that's all that matters." Oprah Winfrey agreed with Betty and said, "That's what I've always believed." Well, I came unglued! That was it! I was enraged! I began yelling at the television and my wife and children ran in to see what all the commotion was about and I had a difficult time collecting myself to even explain it to them. I backed-up the video tape and played it for them and explained that Betty was lying, and that Jesus did not tell her such a falsehood . . . and that there were scriptures to prove it! I reminded my family about what Heavenly Father and Jesus told Joseph Smith in the sacred grove about **all** other religions. Quoting the testimony of the Apostle John, we read: "Jesus answered and said unto him, Verily, verily, I say unto thee, Except a man be born again, he cannot see the kingdom of God . . . (and) Jesus answered, Verily, verily, I say unto thee, Except a man be born of water and of the Spirit, he cannot enter into the Kingdom of God." *(John 3:3, 5.)* It is very clear from much of what the Savior said, that there is much more a person must do here upon the earth to warrant entrance into God's kingdom. This is contrary to what Betty Eadie claims Jesus told her. Would the Lord tell Betty something totally opposite from that which he revealed to His apostles and prophets? Would our Savior tell Betty Eadie something different than what the Holy Scriptures tell us? Of course not!

After I calmed down a bit, I resolved at that very moment to let Betty Eadie and everyone else know just how wrong she is. Betty never did admit on the Oprah Winfrey show that she was a current, baptized member of The Church of Jesus Christ of Latter-day Saints. She refused to admit, stand up and be proud that she was a Mormon. I became very concerned about our tens-of-thousands of Mormon missionaries who would now have this additional obstacle in their path as they proselytize. Why would anyone want to talk to a missionary when they had just witnessed Betty Eadie say she "hugged" Christ and He told her that it didn't matter what church a person belonged to as long as they had love? How about the new converts who are still a little "green" in the gospel principles and maybe somewhat weak in their testimony? When they hear Betty Eadie say that all churches and all faiths and beliefs are true, and that the Lord told her this, what are they to think? This serious damage Betty has caused can never be fully corrected, but it is now time for Betty Eadie and her associate, Curtis

Taylor to publicly recant their false testimonies and tell the truth!

For this reason, I have entitled this expose' *Embarrassed by the Light*. It is not a parody of Betty's *Embraced by the Light*, but it is a definitive answer to the many falsehoods and erroneous information which Betty professes to be truth from God. *Embarrassed by the Light* is a valuable tool by which you, the reader, can successfully compare what Betty alleges to be true and what IS REALLY TRUE! *Embarrassed by the Light* will now "shine the light of truth" on Betty Eadie and expose her motivations, intentions, and hidden agendas for producing the book *Embraced by the Light*.

The fullness of the gospel of Jesus Christ is found within His church, within His scriptures and within the counsel of His apostles and prophets . . . not with Betty and her book! As you read and compare, we ask that you have an open, prayerful heart and you too can experience the truth for yourself. In the revelation known as a preface to the *Doctrine and Covenants*, the Lord says that The Church of Jesus Christ of Latter-day Saints was "the only true and living church upon the face of the whole earth, which, I the Lord, am well pleased." *(D&C 1:30.)*

In preparing this book, *Embarrassed by the Light*, as a clarification of the inequities, falsehoods and errors contained in Eadie's book *Embraced by the light*, I interviewed and polled a large number of people who had read Betty's book. Some were interviewed one-on-one; others were questioned in combined groups and student classes. Males and females; young and old were all involved. It appears that those individuals who believe every word of Betty's tale and those who do not, are evenly split (50/50) on both sides of the fence. Those who disagreed with my view that Betty Eadie and Curtis Taylor were publishing Christian heresy were angry at me for even suggesting that *Embraced by the Light* was an unorthodox view of Mormon thought. They would strike out at me, verbally and with disgust, calling me names and accusing me of un-Christian-like behavior. They refused to listen to my scriptural and doctrinal reasoning. They did not want to hear the truth as taught by the Savior through His prophets here on earth. They had no substantive grounds to support their belief in Betty Eadie, nor could they scripturally provide a reasoning for their support of her book of fantasy and fiction.

Many disgruntled persons asked, "Why would Betty Eadie say and print those things if they weren't true?" I can think of many answers to this question, two motives however, appear as the paramount reason someone could claim a wishful fantasy to be absolute truth. First, is that Betty Eadie's book *Embraced by the Light* has grossed over $20 million! Again, that's $20,000,000.00 in retail book sales in the first 2 years since publication. A pretty great motive to publish a small book, whether it contains the truth or not. Secondly, a combined reason of ego and need to be recognized. Now Betty did not have the greatest childhood a kid could have. Her Scotch-Irish father and her full-blooded Sioux Indian mother were separated when Betty was only four years old. Her father was heard to say that, "Marrying an Indian woman back in those days was probably the worst thing a white man could do." Betty was the seventh of ten children, and six of these children, including Betty, were placed in a Catholic boarding school to be taught and supervised by the Catholic nuns. Betty slept in one large room with 40 other small girls. The nuns cut her hair and de-loused her in chemicals and separated her from her brothers and bigger sisters. *(Embraced . . . , pgs. 3,7.)*

Betty probably needed a large dose of ego boosting after suffering at the hands of her parents, being hit with a rod by Catholic nuns, and then placed in the Brainard Indian Training School which was operated by the Wesleyan Methodists. As a young girl, Betty J. Eadie experienced a mixed variety of Christian teachings. She attended Lutheran church services, Baptist churches and also the Salvation Army. This is the last we read of Betty's religious training. The many, many years she has spent as a baptized member of The Church of Jesus Christ of Latter-day Saints (Mormon) is purposely and conveniently left out. Why would Betty not proudly proclaim that she has been a Mormon for most of her life? What has she to hide? What is she ashamed of? Is she embarrassed to be a Latter-day Saint? A true Christian/Mormon missionary would be proud to proclaim from the tops of the mountains that she was a representative of Jesus Christ . . . and invite all others to join with her! Betty and Curtis did not do that in their book. *(Embraced . . . , pgs. 3,7,10-12.)* The egotistical reasoning behind their publishing of the "Embraced" book of fantasy is serious enough; but the $20,000,000.00 in book sales is still no reason to preach and publish Christian heresy.

If God always reveals His truths and celestial secrets to His prophets *(Amos 3:7)*, then how can Betty Eadie and Curtis Taylor claim to have new insight about the hereafter? This must be a most uncomfortable (even dangerous) position to be in. Do the new Eadie/Taylor revelations invalidate the priesthood authority which has existed since Adam and the beginning of time?

It should be noted that Betty Eadie is a very nice and likable person. She is friendly and comes across as a very gentle, quiet woman in her lectures and in her television interviews. Curtis Taylor was also a very nice, courteous and businesslike gentleman when I saw him at the last LDS Booksellers Association convention in Salt Lake City. Both are highly respected and well thought of individuals, having many friends and close associates. They do not appear to be haughty or high-minded people, but they seem as familiar as your next door neighbor. This can sometimes be a problem when you are asked whether you can trust in a person's integrity or not. Friendliness and familiarity can be deceiving.

That great Prophet Isaiah warned, "And when they shall say unto you, Seek unto them that have familiar spirits, . . . should not a people seek unto their God, for the living to the dead?" *(Isaiah 8:19.)* The Lord cautioned Israel and Judah of such deceptions early in their history when He said: "Regard not them that have familiar spirits, . . . to be defiled by them: I am the Lord." *(Leviticus 10:31.)* "There shall not be found among you any one . . . with familiar spirits . . . For all that do these things are an abomination unto the Lord . . ." *(Deuteronomy 18:10-12.)*

President Joseph Fielding Smith in commenting on these practices gave this warning to us: "To seek for information through . . . any way contrary to the instruction the Lord has given is a sin. The Lord gave positive instruction to Israel when they were in the land of their inheritance that they were to go to Him for revelation and to avoid the devices prevalent among the heathen nations who occupied their lands . . ."

"All through the Bible, the New Testament as well as the Old, the Lord and His prophets have expressed their displeasure when the people turned from the Lord to "familiar spirits." (Joseph Fielding Smith, *Answers to Gospel Questions*, 4:33.)

The purpose of this book is to explain and to document the scriptural inaccuracies and the many fallacies which occur in Betty Eadie's book titled, *Embraced by the Light*.

To all those who are earnestly seeking direction and answers to life's greatest questions — "Who am I? Why am I here? and Where am I going?". . . this book will not only expose Betty's false testimony, but will contain many sacred truths concerning our search for truth and happiness as revealed to His servants the Prophets.

My concern is that readers of the book, *Embraced by the Light* will fully accept everything that Betty Eadie claims is truth, when in fact much of it is blatantly false. Betty and her "ghost writers" have used the basic tenants of the Mormon religion to develop a fantasy, near-death experience which did not actually happen. Many will say, "How can you prove what

Betty Eadie claims did not happen?" The answer to this is very clear. When Betty makes a statement which is contrary to Holy Scripture and prophetic revelation and doctrine, then it must be false.

Much of what Betty states is contrary to the revealed word of Christ. As truth seeking Christians, we must all weigh the truth and the falsehoods in light of sacred and revealed scripture. A half truth is no truth; even dangerously misleading!

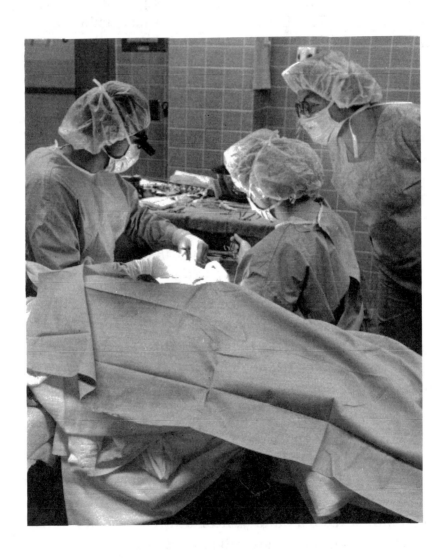

Chapter One

Did Betty Really Die?

I n nationwide broadcast talk show interviews and public relations news releases, Betty has refused to reveal and document her medical and hospital experience. She refuses to submit to a polygraph examination or to ever reveal the name of the doctors, nurses, or hospital to verify even the hint of an actual death experience. If her death actually happened there would be no reason to refuse a quick and simple verification.

Upon interviewing and questioning a number of physicians and anesthesiologists as to what physically occurs at the time of death, the following truths emerge.

After physical death, all of the essential bodily organs die. The brain dies. The heart and lungs die and all of the other vital organs cease to function. Morbidity occurs. The circulatory blood system becomes rigid and incapable of being revived. Betty claims to have actually been dead, not near-death, but dead for over 4 hours. Resuscitation and revival is medically impossible. Lack of oxygen causes brain damage.

Some will say that there are scriptural references and testimonies of individuals who were raised from the dead. This is true; but not without a priesthood administered miracle. There was no priesthood administration which raised Betty Eadie from the dead.

Betty was not in intensive care and she was not electronically monitored by the unknown medical staff of the unknown hospital. This is according to Betty's own written testimony. There were no professional medical personnel to assist her in the event of a sudden death. Her operation was a serious matter. Hysterectomies are a great concern for all women, but hysterectomies do not usually cause death as Betty reports. I am not minimizing the seriousness of this elective surgery, but I am stating that Betty was not in the intensive care of any medical staff, nor were there any family, friends or priesthood brethren with her at the time of her alleged death. There was also no one there when she claims to have returned to life four hours later.

It must be noted that Betty Eadie's alleged death was originally written in a small letter until it was picked up and embellished by a couple of ghost writers, almost 20 years later. Betty admits that there is much of the experience that she has forgotten and could not remember until this later date; almost two decades later.

Mrs. Eadie must be commended for her fine Christian family and for raising children and also for maintaining a continuous marriage to her husband Joe. Christian and humanitarian commendations should also be extended to Betty for avoiding a considered abortion and also for strenuously working to adopt her last child. Her marriage and family, and her celestial decisions to protect the unborn and the helpless children is deserving of praise. This truly was her greatest accomplished mission on earth.

The following clarifications and truthful corrections which are detailed in the following chapters must be prayerfully considered by all truth-seeking Christians and all believers in the wonderful and marvelous life after death as taught and revealed by our Father in Heaven. Please read these pages with an open heart and with a sincere desire to internalize the truth of the glorious eternal life which awaits each of us after death. Eadie's book is not the gospel of Christ.

Betty's final manuscript was enhanced and further embellished by her ghost writer, Curtis Taylor who substantially integrated much of the Mormon doctrine and gospel truths found within the teachings and beliefs of The Church of Jesus Christ of Latter-day Saints headquartered in Salt Lake City, Utah. As a baptized member of the LDS Church, Betty's predominant religious learning and core belief, along with the writing of Curtis Taylor, also a Latter-day Saint, shows subtle hints of the full revealed truth. What is so very disconcerting to the many millions of Mormon members is that Betty Eadie and Curtis Taylor and Jane Barfuss have purposely refused to admit that *The Book of Mormon*, *The Pearl of Great Price*, *The Doctrine and Covenants* and the inspired version of the King James translation of the Old and New Testament is the foundation of their writings in the book *Embraced by the Light*; then they changed the gospel!

The Church of Jesus Christ of Latter-day Saints is recognized as having more detailed truth regarding what awaits all people after death than any other faith and religion on earth. Many Mormons feel that the only reason that Eadie, Taylor and Barfuss refuse to even partially disclose and proudly admit their true beliefs of Mormonism, is that their *Embraced by the Light* book would be rejected by the general public. In other words, no one would purchase the book if proper credit were given to the true church teaching the foundations of their beliefs.

It should be noted that if Betty, Curtis and Jane would now give credit and acknowledge the full truth as revealed by God the Father and God the Son to all the peoples of the earth, that many more of the world's people would understand greater truth of the eternities to come. They would have complete truth in the wondrous after-life that our Father in Heaven has lovingly provided for all the human race.

The prophet Joseph Smith offered us tremendous insight when he said: "Could you gaze into heaven five minutes, you would know more than you would by reading all that ever was written on the subject." Joseph Smith went on to teach, "I assure the Saints that truth, in reference to these matters (death), can and may be known through the revelations of God in the way of His ordinances, and in answer to prayer." *(HC 6:50. Oct. 1843.)*

The Prophet Amos in the Old Testament cautioned us when he said: "Surely the Lord God will do nothing, but he revealeth His secrets unto His servants the prophets." *(Amos 3:7.)* Betty Eadie is not a prophet or prophetess, nor does she claim to be. However, she does claim to reveal many "secrets" and "unknown truths" in her book that have heretofore never been revealed to anyone on earth. Betty claims new enlightenment in our age of darkness about things spiritual, heavenly and celestial; and new revelations about the hereafter that were shown and told to her by our Savior Jesus Christ personally! If this actually occurred, then why did Betty wait two decades to tell it to the world? When Betty did begin to tell her story, Jane Barfuss wrote it in a small 10 page report. It took the work of Curtis Taylor to "grow it" into the 150 page book titled *Embraced by the Light*. Curtis Taylor and Jane Barfuss are not prophets either; nor do they claim to be. Betty, Curtis and Jane were all very surprised and astonished that their book has realized such popularity. That is why **this** book is entitled, *Embarrassed by the Light* because I would personally be embarrassed had I lifted and borrowed Mormon doctrine, then changed and twisted it, then publishing and broadcasting it to the world in order to capitalize upon the desperate search of most men and women for something to believe in and hope for.

When half-truths and falsehood is proclaimed as an actual experience, many people suffer and are actually led into darkness under the disguise of love. Why give only small glimpses of truth when the writers know the whole truth as taught by their own church? Joseph Smith prophetically declared that: "All men know that they must die. And it is important that we understand . . . our departure hence. It is but reasonable to suppose that God would reveal something in reference to the matter, and it is a subject we ought to study more than any other. We ought to study it day and night, for the world is ignorant in reference to their true condition and relation. If we have any claim on our Heavenly Father for anything, it is for knowledge on this important subject (of death). *(HC 6:50.)*

Many individuals who have been under anesthesia have "experienced in their minds" surreal circumstances which were nothing more than sheer fantasy and chemically-induced dreams. Betty Eadie was not even under anesthesia when she claims to have died, or in her words, when she claims to have had a near-death experience. Keep in mind that there is a big difference between near-death and death. Many people have had a near-death experience or a "close-call" with death . . . without actually having died. If you die, your spirit soul actually leaves your mortal, physical body . . . this is not "near-death." It must be one or the other. It cannot be both. Neither can it be a resurrection as Betty details. On the flyleaf of the dust jacket of the book, *Embraced by the Light*, Betty claims to have died and then in the same paragraph claims it was only a near-death experience. What is a reader to believe?

It should be remembered that just because someone believes something has happened to them does not mean that it actually occurred. Who hasn't had a totally realistic dream and then upon awakening discovers that it was a pure and simple fantasy? Realistic, yes . . . but nothing more than a dream conjured up by an active subconscious mind during slumber. Betty claims to be a "hypnotherapist" as printed on the back flyleaf of her book's dust cover. Is Betty able to induce "self-hypnosis?" Only Betty knows.

Hundreds of thousands of human beings died during the same four hours Betty claims to have died and then had her personal, intimate relationship and companionship with our Savior Jesus Christ. Were those thousands of people also met through the "lighted tunnel of love" by our Savior as Betty claims she was? If this were the case, massive hoards of God's children would be traveling homeward at the same time Betty professes to have been there. In addition, pure and innocent baby spirits and souls are returning to the spirit paradise through abortion every year! In order to fully understand the terrible "silent holocaust" and murder that occurs in America today, the numbers break down as follows: over 28,848 abortions each week, or over 5,770 baby deaths every business day, or more than 720 babies killed every working hour in the United States! Shocking! Sinister! The ultimate evil!

Abortion is the greatest evil plaguing the world today. The Lord warned: "And wo be unto man that sheddeth blood or that wasteth flesh and hath no need." *(D&C 49:21.)* Our Lord further condemned those who would abort and kill an innocent unborn baby when He stated: "And now, behold, I speak unto the church. Thou shalt not kill; and he that kills shall not have forgiveness in this world, nor in the world to come. And again, I say, thou shalt not kill; but he that killeth shall die." *(D&C 42:18-19.)*

Many of those who are not in tune with the spirit of the Lord and are unfamiliar with His irrevocable commandments to all peoples of the earth have asked, "If abortion is so evil, why doesn't God stop them from killing unborn babies?" The answer is found in the scriptures *(Alma 14:10-11)* when a similar occurrence happened to the prophets Alma and Amulek in the land of Ammonihah about 82 years before the birth of Christ. As recorded in holy scripture, the two prophets were witnessing the killing of innocent believers in God, and keeping abortion in mind, we read: "And when Amulek saw the pains of the women and children who were consumed in the fire, he also was pained; and he said unto Alma: 'How can we witness this awful scene? Therefore let us stretch forth our hands, and exercise the power of God which is in us, and save them from the flames.'

"But Alma said unto him: 'The Spirit constraineth me that I must not stretch forth mine hand; for behold the Lord receiveth them up unto Himself, in glory; and He doth suffer that they may do this thing, or that the people may do this thing unto them, according to the hardness of their hearts, that the judgments which He shall exercise upon them in His wrath may be just; and the blood of the innocent shall stand as a witness against them in the last day.'" *(Alma 14:10-11.)*

The heinous act of abortion killing is unforgivable according to the words of the Lord. Murder and pre-planned intentional killing was not atoned for by our Savior Jesus Christ. Those individuals who condone, permit and commit abortions will reap the whirlwind of the Lord's vengeance by and by.

There is the possibility that if, in fact, Betty's spirit did leave her body for a short time, that she was confronted by an angel of the Lord. Many thousands of individuals, both Christian and non-Christian have seen and come face-to-face with various types of angels and then have been returned and revived. Some of the angelic beings are relatives or friends who have been assigned by the Lord to greet those souls entering the spirit world. Some angels have been assigned as "guardian angels" to protect and guide us during our sojourn here in mortality.

Angels are a very important part of the gospel of Jesus Christ, particularly in these latter-days. Our most prominent historical edifice, the Salt Lake Temple, has the illustrious Angel Moroni heralding from the tallest spire. Our scriptural standard works are replete with references to the many and mighty works of God and His attending angels.

Our Savior Jesus Christ was attended to by angels during His short life upon the earth. His ministry was intertwined with angels. The birth of Christ was foretold by an angel of God, Gabriel, announcing to Mary that she would give birth to the Messiah. An angel and multitudes of heavenly hosts spread the "good news" of the Savior's birth to the shepherds attending their flocks.

To prepare for the coming of Jesus, the angel Gabriel appeared to Zacharias to inform him that his wife, Elisabeth, would bear a son and that they were to name him John, and that he would be "filled with the Holy Ghost, even from his mother's womb . . . ." *(Luke 1:13, 15.)*

At the end of the forty day and night fast, the devil tried to tempt Jesus with the protection of angels by saying, "If thou be the Son of God, cast thyself down: for it is written, He (God) shall give His angels charge concerning thee: and in their hands they shall bear thee up, lest at any time thou dash thy foot against a stone." *(Matthew 4:6.)* After being tempted three times by Satan, and having resisted temptation and defeated the devil, Jesus was "ministered to by angels." He did not need their help, as He alone won the battle against the tempter, but afterwards the angels came.

In the Garden of Gethsemane, after His disciples had fallen asleep, Jesus kneeled down and prayed saying, "Father, if thou be willing, remove this cup from me: nevertheless not my will, but thine, be done. And there appeared an angel unto Him from Heaven, strengthening Him." *(Luke 22:42-43.)* At which time, the greatest event in the history of the world, and also the most important event in the individual lives of each of us occurred, as Jesus Christ, our Lord and Savior, our Redeemer, took upon Himself and suffered for the sins of the world, as the scripture says: "And being in an agony He prayed more earnestly: and His sweat was as it were great drops of blood falling down to the ground." *(Luke 22:44.)*

Legions of angels were waiting at the cross, available to the Lord should they have been beckoned. An angel announces the resurrection of Jesus, as quoted in Matthew 28:2-4: "And, behold, there was a great earthquake: for the angel of the Lord descended from heaven, and came and rolled back the stone from the door, and sat upon it. His countenance was like lightening, and his raiment white as snow: And for fear of him the keepers did shake, and became as dead men." The angel instructed Mary and the other women to not be afraid, and to witness that Jesus was not in the tomb, and to proceed quickly to tell the other disciples that He had risen from the dead!

In the book of John, chapter 20, verses 11 through 16, we now read how Mary, when she stood outside the sepulchre weeping, looked into the tomb and saw "two angels in white sitting, the one at the head, and the other at the feet, where the body of Jesus had lain. And they say unto her, 'Woman, why weepest thou?'" After Mary explained that she knew not where they had taken her Lord, she turned around and saw Jesus standing before her. Thinking him to be the gardener, she questioned him as she did the two angels at which time she recognized her Master.

There is also the account of the ascension of Jesus in the first chapter of Acts. After He was "taken up," the disciples on Mount Olivet were questioned by two angels in "white apparel," who asked them why they were standing there "gazing up into heaven?"

The restoration of the true Church of Jesus Christ and His power here on earth, the priesthood of God, was all accomplished by the visitation of the Godhead and angelic hosts sent by God. The coming forth of the *Book of Mormon* and its subsequent translation, and, the molding and teaching of the first latter-day prophet, Joseph Smith, was all accomplished by a myriad of angels.

Our Father in Heaven "works in mysterious and wondrous ways" and His "ministering of angels" to man here upon the earth is most wondrous and mysterious.

The Bible Dictionary says that angels are messengers of the Lord, and are spoken of in the epistle to the Hebrews as "ministering angels." Hebrews 1:13-14 records, "But to which of the angels said He at any time, 'Sit on my right hand, until I make thine enemies thy footstools?' Are they not all ministering spirits, sent forth to minister for them who shall be heirs of salvation?" The word "angel" is derived from the Greek word "angelos" which means messenger. Angels are the messengers of our Creator.

We learn from latter-day revelation that there are various classes of heavenly beings who minister for the Lord: those who are spirits and those who have bodies of flesh and bone. Spirits are those beings who either have not yet obtained a body of flesh and bone (unembodied), or who have once had a mortal body and who have died, and are awaiting the resurrection (disembodied).

Ordinarily, the word "angel" means those ministering persons who have a body of flesh and bone, being either resurrected from the dead (reembodied), or else were translated, as were Enoch, Elijah, etc. *(see D&C 129.)* There are many references to the work of angels in the Standard Works. In the scriptures, the word "angel" is found 544 times and is sometimes used to designate human messengers, and there is also scriptural evidence of non-mortal beings, angels, who serve God in the heavens, and also some who do God's will and minister to men on the earth.

Scriptural accounts are cited where angels are called by specific names. In latter-day revelation we learn that the archangel Michael is Adam *(Jude 1:9)*; and that the angel Gabriel is Noah. Modern revelation contains much about the nature, ministry, and identification of angels. We also learn that angels do not have wings. *(History of the Church 3:392.)*

The word "angel" is used in various ways. A person who is a divine messenger is called an angel. Thus Moroni, John the Baptist, Peter, James, John, Moses, Elijah, and Elias all ministered to the Prophet Joseph Smith as angels. These all shall be exalted and inherit celestial glory.

We are told by the Prophet Joseph Smith that "there are no angels who minister to this earth but those who do belong or have belonged to it." Hence, when the messengers are sent to minister to the inhabitants of this earth, they are not strangers, but from the ranks of our kindred, friends, and fellow beings. The ancient prophets who died were those who came to visit their fellow men upon the earth. They came to Abraham, to Isaac, and to Jacob; they were the holy beings who waited upon the Savior and administered to Him upon the Mount. The angel that visited John, when in exile, and unfolded to his vision future events in the history of man upon the earth, was one who had been here, who had toiled and suffered in common with the people of God; for you remember that John, after his eyes had beheld the great glories of the future, was about to fall down and worship him, but was peremptorily forbidden to do so: "See thou do not: for I am thy fellow servant, and of thy brethren the prophets, and of them which keep the sayings of this book: worship God . . ." (*Revelations 22:9.*) It is clear that the scriptures instruct us that we should worship God the Father and our Savior Jesus Christ only; not any of the countless numbers of angels who serve God.

At the funeral services of Elizabeth H. Cannon in Salt Lake City, the Prophet Joseph F. Smith instructed us as recorded in the *Journal of Discourses (Vol. 22, pp. 350-353)* that, "Our fathers and mothers, brothers and sisters and friends who have passed away from this earth, having been faithful, and worthy to enjoy these rights and privileges, may have a mission given to them to visit their relatives and friends upon the earth again, bringing from the Divine Presence messages of love, of warning, or of reproof and instruction to those whom they had learned to love in the flesh. And so it is with Sister Cannon. She can return and visit her friends, provided it be in accordance with the wisdom of the Almighty.

"There are laws to which they who are in the Paradise of God must be subject, as well as laws to which we are subject. It is our duty to make ourselves acquainted with those laws, that we may know how to live in harmony with His will while we dwell in the flesh, that we may be entitled to come forth in the morning of the first resurrection, clothed with glory, immortality and eternal lives, and be permitted to sit down at the right hand of God, in the kingdom of heaven.

"And except we become acquainted with those laws, and live in harmony with them, we need not expect to enjoy these privileges. Joseph Smith, Hyrum Smith, Brigham Young, Heber C. Kimball, Jedediah M. Grant, David Patten, Joseph Smith, Sr., and all those noble men who took an active part in the establishment of this work, and who died true and faithful to their trust, have the right and privilege, and possess the keys and power, to minister to the people of God in the flesh who live now, as much so, and on the same principle as the ancient servants of God had the right to return to the earth and minister to the saints of God in their day.

"These are correct principles. There is no question about that in my mind. It is according to the scriptures; it is according to the revelation of God to the Prophet Joseph Smith; and it is a subject upon which we may dwell with pleasure and perhaps profit to ourselves, provided we have the Spirit of God to direct us." *(Joseph F. Smith, Sixth President and Prophet of The Church of Jesus Christ of Latter-day Saints.)*

At the time wicked King Herod killed (with a sword) the Apostle James, the brother of John, and Herod seeing that the Jews were pleased with this murder, imprisoned Peter to do likewise unto him. Herod apprehended Peter and delivered him into the hands of 16 soldiers to be imprisoned and executed after Easter. After much unceasing prayer offered up unto God by the members of the Church, the following is a scriptural account of what Peter's "guardian angel" did for his protection as directed by the Lord: "And when Herod would have brought him forth (to execute), the same night Peter was sleeping between two soldiers, bound with two chains: and the keepers before the door of the prison.

"And, behold, the angel of the Lord came upon him, and a light shined in the prison: and he smote Peter on the side, and raised him up, saying, 'Arise up quickly.' And his chains fell off his hands.

"And the angel said unto him, 'Gird thyself, and bind on thy sandals.' And so he did. And he saith unto him, 'Cast thy garment about thee, and follow me.'

"And he went out, and followed him; and wist not that it was true that was done by the angel; but thought he saw a vision.

"When they were past the first and the second ward, they came unto the iron gate that leadeth unto the city; which opened to them of his own accord: and they went out, and passed through one street; and forthwith the angel departed from him.

"And when Peter had come to himself, he said, 'Now I know of a surety, that the Lord hath sent His angel, and hath delivered me out of the hand of Herod, and from all the expectation of the people of the Jews.'" *(Acts 12:6-11.)*

Miraculous to say the least! Unshackled wrist chains, iron gates opened, past many guards and freed from the dark prison of death; what a mighty angelic deliverance Peter testifies of receiving at the hand of the Lord, providing additional time for Peter to lead the ancient Church.

In the Psalms we read, "He that dwelleth in the secret place of the most High shall abide under the shadow of the Almighty. For He shall give His angels charge over thee, to keep thee in thy ways. They shall bear thee up in their hands, lest thou dash thy foot against a stone." *(Psalms 91:1,11,12.)*

Every true believer in Christ should be encouraged and uplifted and strengthened! Angels are watching and they mark our paths. Angels superintend the events of our lives and they protect the interests of the Lord; always working to promote and bring to pass God's highest will for us. Angels are our interested spectators and mark all that we do: ". . . for we are made a spectacle unto the world, and to angels, and to me." *(1 Corinthians 4:9.)* Heavenly Father assigns angelic powers to watch over us, delegating others to record and keep our celestial records as we proceed through our examination here on earth. Angels are keepers of our collective personal histories.

Even in infancy, our individual guardian angels are with us, as Jesus said, "Take heed that ye despise not one of these little ones; for I say unto you, that in heaven their angels do always behold the face of my Father which is in heaven." *(Matthew 18:10.)*

Visions, dreams and revelations experienced by our Heavenly Father's holy prophets and others, who describe what appear to be wings on angels, may simply be viewing the wondrous "flowing robes" and "celestial garments" made of the most exquisite white and bright materials, giving the appearance of "angel wings" as they travel in the heavens. We know from the scriptures and from the personal testimonies of those who have seen our Father in Heaven and His son Jesus Christ, that spirits and angels and each of us are made in the "image of God" and we do not have wings, nor do we need wings.

Ministering angels probably know more about us than we know about ourselves, and their power is far superior to that of ours. Their "angelic vision" is enhanced and magnified by their ability to pierce the unseen heavenly veil which exists between our world and the spirit world. Paul refers to the "mighty angels" of God in 2 Thessalonians 1:7. David speaks of the Lord's angels "that excel in strength, that do His commandments, hearkening unto the voice of His word." Knowledge, strength, power and righteousness are all "angelic attributes" that each of us must strive to possess in order to mold ourselves into effective tools in the hands of the Lord.

We cannot study the subject of angels in the scriptures without becoming aware of "fallen angels" or "dark angels" who were not valiant spirits in the preexistence. In *Revelation 12:7-9*, we read, "And there was war in heaven; Michael and his angels fought against the dragon; and the dragon fought and his angels, and prevailed not; neither was their place found any more in heaven. And the great dragon was cast out, that old serpent, called the Devil, and Satan, which deceiveth the whole world: he was cast out into the earth, and his angels were cast out with him."

Here we see that Satan and his followers, or a third of the angels of heaven were cast out and became "devils." The Apostle Peter said, "God spareth not the angels that sinned, but cast them down to hell, and delivered them into the chains of darkness, to be reserved unto judgement." *(2 Peter 2:4.)* These spirit angels "kept not their first estate" *(see Jude 6)* and as such, were cast down and became "devils" who now seek to thwart our best and most righteous endeavors as we work to progress the gospel here upon the earth.

The Prophet Joseph Smith received a revelation in September of 1830 which is recorded in Doctrine & Covenants 29:36-38: "And it came to pass that Adam, being tempted of the devil, for behold, the devil was before Adam, for he rebelled against Me, saying, 'Give Me thine honor, which is My power;' and also a third part of the hosts of heaven turned he away from Me because of their agency. And they were thrust down, and thus became the devil and his angels. And, behold, there is a place prepared for them from the beginning, which place is hell."

It is not wrong to expect the spirit of God, the Holy Ghost and powerful angels to accompany you in your many life experiences. Live righteously, obey the commandments and covenants of the Lord and you can expect to be protected and watched over always. Realizing that there are spirit angels in an unseen world constantly watching us is an excellent incentive to "choose the right!" *(1 Corinthians 4:9.)*

Angels are nearer than you think. For after all, Heavenly Father has given "His angels charge over thee, to keep thee in all thy ways." We should always be grateful for the goodness and mercy of God, who uses these wonderful friends called "angels" to guide and protect us. Evidences from the scriptures, as well as personal experience, confirms to us that individual guardian and guiding angels attend our ways and watch over our lives. Psalms 34:7 emphasizes the teaching and truth that angels do protect and deliver the people of God: "The angel of the Lord encampeth round about them that fear Him, and delivereth them."

Chapter Two

Who Should Judge Betty?

Matthew 7:1 reads: "Judge not, that ye be not judged." Some will say, "Aren't you judging when you call Betty a fake?"

First, in order to answer this question we must ask, "Is Jesus teaching that a Christian should never express an opinion about others?" Should a Christian be easy-going, indulgent and tolerant, and allow any view at all to pass for the sake of unity?

If Matthew 7:1 says, "Judge not . . . ," verse 6 says, "Give not that which is holy unto the dogs, neither cast ye your pearls before swine, lest they trample them under feet . . ." How can a Christian know which kind of person can be described as a "dog" or "swine" if he does not think and exercise judgment? In other words, the injunction immediately following this command to not judge, at once demands that we exercise righteous judgment.

A few verses later, Jesus states, "Beware of false prophets which come to you in sheep's clothing, but inwardly they are ravening wolves." *(Matthew 7:15.)* How can a true Christian beware of false prophets if he never makes an assessment of a person's teachings? Our Savior warned us that these people will come in sheep's clothing—that is, they are very warm, personable, likable people, and they use Christian terminology. Betty Eadie and her "ghost writers" do this very well. They appear to be very harmless and honest and are invariably "nice and loving." But if we are to obey our Lord, we must not be taken in by those who proclaim fantasy as reality or falsehood for the truth. And if we are not to be taken in by them, we must compare all that they claim to be true with the teachings and revelations of Jesus and the apostles.

In Matthew 7:16-20, Jesus tells us,

"Ye shall know them by their fruits . . . Even so every good tree bringeth forth good fruit; but a corrupt tree bringeth forth evil fruit. A good tree cannot bring forth evil fruit, neither can a corrupt tree bring forth good fruit. Every tree that bringeth not forth good fruit is hewn down, and cast into the fire. Wherefore by their fruits ye shall know them."

We challenge Betty Eadie and Curtis Taylor to truthfully and openly admit that they twisted the Mormon teachings and scripture when they crafted their "Embraced" novel. They should be honest enough with the public to confess and disclose their hidden agenda.

The verses in Matthew chapter 7 clearly show that in saying "Judge not," Jesus isn't teaching that we are not to think, or examine, or differentiate between true and false views. On the contrary, we must exercise judgement if we are to obey our Lord's commands. But then, what is Jesus teaching when he says, "Do not judge?" Jesus is warning of a "certain kind" of judging—one that is not based on examining the evidence, but is based on a wrong attitude or a critical spirit. Jesus is warning us not to pass judgement based on prejudiced feelings that elicit a conclusion from us about someone or something before objectively examining the evidence.

Jesus is talking about a hypercritical spirit which judges unjustly, which pronounces judgements stemming from pride, jealousy, revenge—a heart that is happy to hurt someone, that is quick to condemn another person apart from the facts. This is the kind of judgement that Jesus says we are not to do as Christians. He is not teaching us that we should give up thinking and judging the true from the false prophets, or the scriptural teachings from the false teachings. Knowing the truth obligates us, as true Christians, to warn and to persuade and to prevent others from following error. The Savior requires us to make proper judgements every day. We read in Moroni 7:16-17 about our ability to discern and judge good from evil: "For behold, the spirit of Christ is given to every man, that he may know good from evil; wherefore, I show unto you the way to judge: for every good thing which inviteth to do good, and to persuade to believe in Christ, is sent forth by the power and gift of Christ; wherefore ye may know with a perfect knowledge it is of God. But whatsoever thing persuadeth men to do evil, and believe not in Christ, and deny him, and serve not God, then ye may know with a perfect knowledge it is of the devil; for after this manner doth the devil work, for he persuadeth no man to do good, no, not one; neither do his angels; neither do they who subject themselves unto him."

Betty Eadie would have us believe that she was embraced and held in the arms of our Lord Jesus Christ! Let's read what He says about this. Jehovah, who is Jesus Christ, and God of the Old Testament, spoke to the Prophet Moses, "And He said, 'Thou canst not see My face: for there shall no man see Me, and live.'" *(Exodus 33:20.)* The mother and father of Samson saw an angel sent by the Lord and believing that they had actually seen God, "And Manoah said to his wife, 'We shall surely die, because we have seen God.'" *(Judges 13:22.)* If the righteous throughout time understood that seeing God resulted in death (as they were told by the Lord) then how can Betty claim to have been "embraced" by the Lord? It is simply not true. Maybe a wish or a dream on Betty's part, but not reality according to the Lord and His scriptures and His prophets. When the Lord spoke to the brother of Jared, He said, "And never have I showed Myself unto man whom I have created, for never has man believed in Me as thou hast." *(Ether 3:15.)*

The fantastic claim of Betty Eadie and Curtis Taylor should be viewed in light of what God revealed to Moses when He said: "Wherefore, no man can behold all My works, except he behold all My glory; and no man can behold all My glory, and afterwards remain in the flesh on earth." *(Moses 1:5.)*

Elder Bruce R. McConkie illuminated what happens after death in this wonderful way:

"I shall speak of a subject which strikes dread—even terror—into the hearts of men. It is something we fear, of which we are sorely afraid, and from which most of us would flee if we could.

"I shall speak of the passing of the immortal soul into the eternal realms ahead, of that dreaded day when we shall shuffle off this mortal coil and go back to the dust from whence we came. I shall speak of death—mortal death, the natural death, the death of the body—and of the state of the souls of men when this final consummation is imposed upon them.

"Manifestly, we must all be guided and enlightened by the power of the Holy Spirit as we step into this realm, this realm of which carnal men know so little, but of which so much has been revealed to the saints of the Most High.

"I pray that my words shall sink deeply into your hearts by the power of that same spirit, so that you will know of their truth and verity.

"For a text I take these sweet and consoling words of biblical origin: 'Precious in the sight of the Lord is the death of His saints.' *(Psalms 116:15.)* To them I append Paul's pointed and painful pronouncement: 'The sting of death is sin.' *(1 Cor. 15:56.)*

"Death can be comforting and sweet and precious or it can thrust upon us all the agonies and sulphurous burnings of an endless hell. And we—each of us individually—make the choice as to which it shall be.

"If we are to place death in its proper perspective in the eternal scheme of things, we must first learn the purposes of life. We must know whence we came, whose we are and why He placed us here. Only then can we envision whither we shall yet go in the providences of Him who made us.

"We know, because the Lord has revealed it in this our day, that we are the spirit children of an exalted, glorified Being, a Holy Man who has a body of flesh and bones and who is our Father in heaven.

"We know that the name of the kind of life He lives is eternal life and that it consists of living in the family unit and of possessing all power, all might and all dominion.

"We know that He ordained and established the plan of salvation to enable us to advance and progress from our spirit state, to the same state of glory, honor and exaltation which He Himself possesses.

"We know that the Father's plan called for the creation of this earth, where we could dwell as mortals, receive bodies made of the dust of the earth, and undergo the tests and trials which now face us.

"We know that this plan of salvation included provisions for the fall of man, with its consequent temporal spiritual death; for a redemption from death through the atoning sacrifice for the Son of God; and for an inheritance of eternal life for all the obedient.

"We know that this great plan of progression called for a birth which would provide a mortal tabernacle for our eternal spirits, and for a death which would free those spirits from the frailties, diseases, and weaknesses of mortality.

"And may I say that this life never was intended to be easy. It is a probationary estate in which we are tested physically, mentally, morally, and spiritually. We are subject to disease and decay. We are attacked by cancer, illness, and contagious diseases. We suffer pain and sorrow and afflictions. Disasters strike; floods sweep away our homes; famines destroy our food; plagues and wars fill our graves with dead bodies and our broken homes with sorrow.

"We are called upon to choose between the revealed word of God and the soul-destroying postulates of the theoretical sciences. Temptations, the lusts of the flesh, evils of every sort—all these are part of the plan, and must be faced by every person privileged to undergo the experiences of mortality.

"The testing processes of mortality are for all men, saints and sinners alike. Sometimes the tests and trials of those who have received the gospel far exceed any imposed upon worldly people. Abraham was called upon to sacrifice his only son. Lehi and his family left their lands and wealth to live in a wilderness. Saints in all ages have been commanded to lay all that they have upon the altar, sometimes even their very lives.

"As to the individual trials and problems that befall any of us, all we need say is that in the wisdom of Him who knows all things, and who does all things well, all of us are given the particular and specific tests that we need in our personal situations. It is to us, His saints, that the Lord speaks when He says, 'I will prove you in all things, whether you will abide in My covenant, even unto death, that you may be found worthy.

"For if ye will not abide in My covenant ye are not worthy of Me. *(D&C 98:14-15.)*

"Now, what of death? Of the passing of loved ones? Of our life beyond the grave?

"Our scriptures say: 'Death hath passed upon all men, to fulfill the merciful plan of the Great Creator.' *(2 Nephi 9:6.)* Where the true saints are concerned, there is no sorrow in death except that which attends a temporary separation from loved ones. Birth and death are both essential steps in the unfolding drama of eternity.

"We shouted for joy at the privilege of becoming mortal because without the test of mortality there could be no eternal life. We now sing praises to the great Redeemer for the privilege of passing from this life, because without death and the resurrection we could not be raised in immortal glory and gain eternal life.

"When the faithful saints depart from this life, they 'are received into a state of happiness, which is called paradise, a state of rest, a state of peace, where they shall rest from all their troubles and from all care, and sorrow' *(Alma 40:12)*, and they remain in this state until the day of their resurrection.

"When the wicked and ungodly depart from this life they continue in their wickedness and rebellion. 'That same spirit which doth possess your bodies at the time ye go out of this life,' the scripture says, 'that same spirit will have power to possess your body in that eternal world.' *(Alma 34:34.)*

"'Ye must press forward with a steadfastness in Christ,' Nephi said to members of the Church, 'having a perfect brightness of hope, and a love of God and of all men. Wherefore, if ye shall press forward, feasting upon the word of Christ, and endure to the end, behold, thus saith the Father: Ye shall have eternal life.' *(2 Nephi 31:20.)* That is to say—all the faithful saints, all of those who have endured to the end, depart this life with the absolute guarantee of eternal life.

"There is no equivocation, no doubt, no uncertainty in our minds. Those who have been true and faithful in this life will not fall by the wayside in the life to come. If they keep their covenants here and now, and depart from this life firm and true in the testimony of our blessed Lord, they shall come forth with an inheritance of eternal life.

"We do not mean to say that those who die in the Lord, and who are true and faithful in this life, must be perfect in all things when they go into the next sphere of existence. There was only one perfect—the Lord Jesus whose Father was God.

"There have been many righteous souls who have attained relative degrees of perfection, and there have been great hosts of faithful people who kept the faith, and lived the law, and departed this life with the full assurance of an eventual inheritance of eternal life.

"There are many things they will do and must do, even beyond the grave, to merit the fullness of the Father's kingdom in that final glorious day when the great King shall say unto them, 'Come, ye blessed of My Father, inherit the kingdom prepared for you from the foundations of the world.' *(Matthew 25:34.)*

"But what we are saying is that when the saints of God chart a course of righteousness, when they gain sure testimonies of the truth and divinity of the Lord's work, when they keep the commandments, when they overcome the world, when they put first in their lives the things of God's kingdom: when they do all these things, and then depart this life—though they have not yet become perfect—they shall nonetheless gain eternal life in our Father's kingdom; and eventually they shall be perfect as God, their Father, and Christ, His Son, are perfect.

"Is it any wonder that the scriptures say: 'Precious in the sight of the Lord is the death of His saints.' *(Psalms 116:15.)* Truly such is precious, wondrous, and glorious, for when the saints die, added souls have assured themselves of exaltation with Him who provided the way for them to advance and progress and become like Him.

"Is it any wonder that the scriptures say: 'Blessed are the dead which die in the Lord, for they shall rest from their labours; and their works do follow them.' *(Rev. 14:13.)* Truly it is a blessed occasion, for the faithful saints who have filled the full measure of their creation, and a gracious God will give them all things in due course.

"Is it any wonder that the Lord says to His saints, 'Those that die in Me shall not taste of death, for it shall be sweet unto them?' *(D&C 42:46.)*

"Is it any wonder that the Prophet Joseph Smith said such things as: 'When men are prepared, they are better off to go hence.' *(Teachings of the Prophet Joseph Smith, pg. 326.)*

"'Those who have died in Jesus Christ may expect to enter into all that fruition of joy when they come forth, which they possessed or anticipated here.' *(Teachings, pg. 295.)*

"'In the resurrection, some are raised to be angels, others are raised to become Gods.' *(Teachings*, pg. 312.)

"Now, we do not seek death, though it is part of the merciful plan of the Great Creator. Rather, we rejoice in life, and desire to live as long as we can be of service to our fellowmen. Faithful saints are a leaven of righteousness in a wicked world.

"But sometimes the Lord's people are hounded and persecuted. Sometimes He deliberately lets His faithful saints linger and suffer, in both body and spirit, to prove them in all things, and to see if they will abide in His covenant, even unto death, that they may be found worthy of eternal life. If such be the lot of any of us, so be it.

"But come what may, anything that befalls us here in mortality is but for a small moment, and if we are true and faithful, God will eventually exalt us on high. All our losses and sufferings will be made up to us in the resurrection.

"We shall be raised from mortality to immortality, from corruption to incorruption. We shall come forth from the grave in physical perfection. Not a hair of the head shall be lost, and God shall wipe away all the tears.

"If we have lived the gospel we shall come forth with celestial bodies which are prepared to stand the glory of a celestial kingdom. We shall continue to live in the family unit, and as Joseph Smith said, 'That same society which exists among us here will be coupled with eternal glory, which glory we do not now enjoy!' *(D&C 130:2.)*

"Oh, that it might be with each of us as it was with that valiant apostle of old who said, as the hour of his death approached:

"'I am ready to be offered, and the time of my departure is at hand.

"'I have fought a good fight, I have finished my course, I have kept the faith:

"'Henceforth there is laid up for me a crown of righteousness, which the Lord, the righteous judge, shall give me at that day: and not unto me only, but unto all them also that love His appearing.'" *(2 Tim. 4:6-8) (Bruce R. McConkie, Passage to Light.* 1979, pgs. 125-132.)

Chapter Three

What About Christian Tolerance?

Aren't Christians supposed to be tolerant? Tolerance for some is like a garbage can. They accept everything and anything! For others, tolerance may camouflage a lack of courage to commit to one's self. Practiced still by others, it leads to the most rigid intolerance. For example, there are those whose passion for tolerance makes them totally intolerant of anyone who has conviction.

Does tolerance mean that a true Christian is never to take a stand for anything? Are we to be always without convictions and principles? Obviously not! Then it would seem that no one should say a Christian is intolerant because he or she takes their convictions seriously.

Intolerance is the acid test of character. Scripturally, it is right to be intolerant of evil, greed, selfishness, pride, injustice, oppression, falsehood and anything that violates the teachings of God. The trouble with some people is that nothing makes them mad! They will coexist with anything no matter how it outrages truth and righteousness. They call for unity and tranquility and are willing to compromise any truths to attain it. Jesus Christ was love incarnate, but He never made a "deal" with the enemies of righteousness. He died for sinners, but He never compromised with sinners!

Every Christian should personally examine and pray to receive a witness of the truth. Those who do will emerge from the experience a better person, more sure of the reliability of the prophet, apostles and scriptures as the only rule and guide to the everlasting life with God in the celestial kingdom. Some have said, "Wasn't Betty trying to do good when she pretended to visit with Jesus?"

The Apostle Paul told the Galatians: "I marvel that ye are so soon removed from him that called you into the grace of Christ from another gospel: which is not another, but there be some that trouble you, and would pervert the gospel of Christ. But though we, or an angel from heaven, preach any other gospel unto you than that which we have preached unto you, let him be accursed." *(Galatians 1:6-9.)* Betty Eadie and Curtis Taylor have "perverted the gospel of Christ" and have published, distributed and "preached another gospel" just as Paul warned us in the New Testament.

Many early Christians were upset and angry at the Apostle Paul because he preached the truth. Paul was very intolerant of false, perverted and twisted teachings. Sensing that anger, he asked: "Am I therefore your enemy, because I tell you the truth?" *(Galatians 4:16.)* Paul further stated that, ". . . it is good to be zealously affected always in a good thing . . ." *(Galatians 4:18.)* It is plain to see that we are commanded to be "zealously intolerant" of anything and everything that is contrary to the true teachings of Christ. Silence on such matters could be construed as a sinful omission by lack of action and conviction to the truth.

The very title of the book boldly states that Betty Eadie was actually "embraced by the light," or in other words, she claims to have been "embraced by the Savior!" This is blasphemy . . . a mockery of God. The Apostle Paul told the Christians in Galatia to: "Be not deceived; God is not mocked; for whatsoever a man soweth, that shall he also reap." *(Galatians 6:7.)*

The true plan of salvation as outlined by our Father in Heaven was totally ignored in Betty's and Curtis' book. The specific priesthood ordinances which Jesus Christ taught and revealed as necessary pertaining to entrance into the celestial kingdom were missing from the "Embraced" book. They failed miserably to explain and warn their readers as to the essential priesthood administered ordinances necessary for entrance into Christ's celestial presence. Betty tries to make the case that as long as you love one another, that this is all that is needed to "embrace Jesus." This teaching is misleading and wrong. God's prophets and the scriptures dispute Betty's erroneous testimony.

Jacob, the prophet, cautioned us by asking these very deep and probing questions: "Behold, will ye reject these words? Will ye reject the words of the prophets; and will ye reject all the words which have been spoken concerning Christ, after so many have spoken concerning Him; and deny the good word of Christ, and the power of God, and the Gift of the Holy Ghost, quench the Holy Spirit, and make a mock of the great plan of redemption, which hath been laid for you?" *(Jacob 6:8.)* The great plan of life, salvation and redemption has already been laid before us by the Savior. Betty's plan is incomplete and untrue!

Our beloved apostle, N. Eldon Tanner talked about the plan of life and salvation when he wrote this touching message to us:

"Recently, we mourned the passing of a beloved friend, colleague, and brother, who had spent many years of his life in the service of his Maker and his fellowmen. He contributed greatly to the community, the Church, and industry. He was a good friend and neighbor. At his funeral we heard one of his favorite songs, which he had sung so well and so often:

> I know that my Redeemer lives;
> What comfort this sweet sentence gives!
> He lives, He lives, who once was dead.
> He lives, my ever-living head . . .
> O Sweet the joy this sentence gives:
> 'I know that my Redeemer lives!'
> *(Hymns, no. 136.)*

"The passing of loved ones has always caused us to stop and ponder such questions as:

> Who am I?
> Where did I come from?
> Why am I here?
> Where am I going?
> How can I best prepare myself?

"I am sure that thousands and thousands have said, 'If I knew the answers to these questions, I would know better how to govern my life.' It is impossible for any of us, including philosophers, astrologers, astronomers, and scientists in any field, with our finite minds, to answer these questions pertaining to the infinite without referring to the word of God as contained in the scriptures.

"We mortals have never experienced death and the resurrection, nor do we remember our pre-existence. Therefore, it is not commonly believed or understood that we had a premortal existence, that we are the spirit children of God, the Eternal Father, and that when we have finished our life here upon the earth we will enjoy a literal resurrection and may continue on in eternal progression. In fact, many who question this say that if someone would return from the dead as a witness of these things, they would believe. This is not so.

"Let us remember the parable of the rich man who prayed that Lazarus be sent from the dead to his father's house to testify to his brethren, saying that if one went to them from the dead, they would repent. Abraham said unto him: 'If they hear no Moses and the prophets, neither will they be persuaded, though one rose from the dead.'" (*Luke 16:31.*)

"How fortunate we are that the Lord God, from the time of Adam, down through the ages to the present time, has given us the answers to these very important questions, and we have them recorded in Holy Writ. Yes, God has seen fit to talk to His people through His chosen prophets, and those who have heard and believed and followed have been blessed.

"It is sad but true that many, many people are not acquainted with the words of the prophets, and many refuse to believe, and others often scoff and ridicule the teachings of the Savior. It is extremely sad that many, through their own learning and their sensuous knowledge, become self-satisfied and think that they are sufficient unto themselves and need not heed the word of God; and often, because they have not heard, seen, touched, or talked to God, they deny even His very existence, and use their influence to dissuade others.

"But all of this ignorance, derision, scoffing, and ridicule does not destroy the truth, which finally will triumph. We must learn to live by faith and believe in the words of the Lord, especially in those things which we mortals do not and cannot fully comprehend. Probably the greatest evidence of the fact that God speaks to His prophets is the fulfillment of the prophecies made by them. Many of these prophecies and their fulfillment are a matter of historical and scriptural record.

"As I was pondering the questions to which I have referred, and their answers, and in turning to the scriptures I quote again this significant and most important statement:

'And this is life eternal, that they might know thee the only true God, and Jesus Christ, whom thou has sent.' (*John 17:3.*)

"Many ask: 'How can a man know God and Jesus Christ, whom He has sent?' The answer must be clear that it is through prayer and faith and study of the works of God as given through His prophets and by Jesus Christ, whom He has sent. Let us refer to some revelations received and prophecies made by both ancient and modern prophets that tell us about God and our relationship to Him, and that will help us to know and understand the purpose of our mission here on earth.

"Probably the very earliest scriptural account we have of man and his relationship to God, and which shows beyond doubt that we had a premortal existence in the spirit world with God, is the record of the council in heaven as revealed to Moses and Abraham.

'Now the Lord has shown unto me, Abraham, the intelligences that were organized before the world was; . . .

'And God . . . stood in the midst of them, and He said: These I will make My rulers; for He stood among those that were spirits, . . . and He said unto me: Abraham, thou art one of them; thou wast chosen before thou wast born.

'And there stood one among them that was like unto God, and He said unto those who were with Him: We will go down for there is space there' . . . (*P of GP 3:22-24.*) The Sermon on the Mount, and the whole plan of life and salvation-the blueprint of life-which if lived will not only bring joy to us here on earth but will prepare us for immortality and eternal life, where we can dwell with God the Father and his Son Jesus Christ and our loved ones who have gone there before us.

"Our Heavenly Father, knowing our weaknesses and our need for constant direction, sends us prophets to continually teach us and keep us reminded of this plan of life and salvation. Our salvation and that of our loved ones depends on our listening to and heeding the words of the prophets, realizing that we must believe all that God has revealed, all that He does now reveal, and that He will yet reveal many great and important things pertaining to the kingdom of God.

"To those who question these things, I should like to emphasize this one fact: Everything that was taught by the prophets and by Jesus Christ himself, as recorded in Holy Writ, is for the benefit of mankind, and if accepted and lived will make for better individuals, better communities, a better world where we can live in love and peace with one another.

"Man by his own formula has failed to accomplish these things. He has no effective plan, and any failure is because man has failed to live its teachings. To those who doubt or question, but have no answers, and who look for hope out of the midst of their despair, I urge that they accept the work of God the Eternal Father and believe in the gospel, which is uplifting and beautiful and will bring peace and contentment to their souls. How much better to hope than despair, and the works of hope and everlasting life with the Father and the Son are to be found in the gospel of Jesus Christ.

"He summed it all up and gave a simple formula when He answered the lawyer who asked, tempting Him:

"Master, which is the great commandment in the law?

"Jesus said unto him, Thou shalt love the Lord thy God with all thy heart, and with all thy soul, and with all thy mind.

"This is the first and great commandment.

"And the second is like unto it, Thou shalt love thy neighbor as thyself.

"On these two commandments hang all the law and the prophets." *(Matt. 22:36-40.)*

The Lord also said that if we love Him, we will keep His commandments. These are the teachings of all the apostles and prophets. Let us heed the words of Peter as he was speaking to and answered the multitude:

"Now when they heard this, they were pricked in their heart, and said unto Peter and to the rest of the apostles, 'Men and brethren, what shall we do?'

"Then Peter said unto them, Repent and be baptized every one of you in the name of Jesus Christ for the remission of sins, and ye shall receive the gift of the Holy Ghost.

"For the promise is unto you, and to your children, and to all that are afar off, even as many as the Lord our God shall call." *(Acts 2:37-39.)*

"It is important to understand that we are here to prove ourselves, to prepare ourselves to go back into the presence of our Heavenly Father, and the choices we make will determine our future happiness. Hear the words of the American prophet Lehi to his sons, which message has been given repeatedly to the children of men through the ages:

"Wherefore, men are free according to the flesh; and all things are given them which are expedient unto man. And they are free to choose liberty and eternal life or to choose captivity and death, according to the captivity and power of the devil; for he seeketh that all men might be miserable like unto himself.

"And now, my sons, I would that ye should look to the great Mediator, and hearken unto His great commandments; and be faithful unto His works and choose eternal life, according to the will of His Holy Spirit:

"And not choose eternal death, according to the will of the flesh and the evil which is therein, which giveth the spirit of the devil power to captivate, to bring you down to hell, that he may reign over you in his own kingdom." *(2 Ne. 2:27-29.)*

"Jacob, Lehi's son, taught: "Therefore, cheer up your hearts, and remember that ye are free to act for yourselves-to choose the way of everlasting death or the way of eternal life.'" *(2 Ne. 10:23.)*

To summarize, we read from Ecclesiastes: "Let us hear the conclusion of the whole matter. Fear God, and keep His commandments; for this is the whole duty of man." *(Eccl. 12:13.)* (N. Eldon Tanner, *Passage to Light*, 1979, pgs. 99-105.)

Much of the book *Embraced by the Light* is senseless drivel, and much of the book is very damaging. It is not possible to fully comment on each and every paragraph in Betty's and Curtis' book, but it is important and necessary to examine some of the most questionable, erroneous and blatantly untrue segments. Betty and Curtis are gospel "spin-doctors!"

Chapter Four

Hypnotism and the "Eadie-ites"

T here have been so many Mormons and other Christians who have "bought" Betty Eadie's and Curtis Taylor's ideas of new-age religion that many are now calling Betty's believers, EADIE-ITES! Not "idiots," but "Eadie-ites." The best definition of the so called, Eadie-ites is a person (Christian or non-Christian) who proclaims a belief in Betty Eadie's "spin" on the teachings of the hereafter, instead of the Lord's teachings as found in the scriptures.

On page 37 of *Embraced by the Light,* Betty described her death as "a very pleasant feeling—almost hypnotic. I heard chimes, or distant bells, tinkling. . . . Darkness began to surround my being . . . I was drawn up and into a great, whirling, black mass . . . as if I had been swallowed up by an enormous tornado . . . I felt a profoundly pleasant sense of well being and calmness." *(Embraced,* pgs. 37-38.)

Betty Eadie is a self-proclaimed "hypnotist" or hypnotherapist. (see back cover, fly-leaf; second paragraph of "Embraced") Betty dropped out of high school and got married at the age of 15 and then completed her GED requirements many years later. As a hypnotist/hypnotherapist, Ms. Eadie would know how to perform self-hypnosis and would be able to place herself in a "hypnotic trance" at will; any time she chose to do so. It also seems that the many Eadie-ites who find it easier and prefer to blindly believe and follow Betty and Curtis are hypnotized as well. The Eadie-ites prefer to believe and follow Betty and Curtis instead of discovering the real truth for themselves by prayerfully studying the scriptures and feasting on the word of God as taught by His holy prophets.

Hypnotism has no place in Christianity! In his masterful book, titled *Overcoming Satan in the Latter Days*, Timothy Wood thoroughly discusses hypnotism and is herein quoted: "I was introduced to hypnotism through the movies and TV. 'You're falling asleep . . . you're getting sleepy . . . you're under my power,' droned Count Dracula. 'Yes, Master,' was the reply. The hypnotized would obey the slightest command. With this awesome power at my fingertips I went to the library and started reading books on the subject. I discovered that what the world calls hypnotism today has been regarded as a mysterious force or spell throughout the history of man. Scientists have many theories, but they cannot explain how it works, or why. Movies and books show its beneficial effects upon medicine, for painless surgery and childbirth, psychiatric treatments and as an aid in overcoming bad habits such as smoking, drugs and drinking.

"To become hypnotized, one must volunteer to allow themselves to be put into a state of sleep, similar to the kind of sleep we experience each night. We sleep over one-third of our life away. How do we fall asleep? What happens to our mind when we slumber?

"Simply put, the spirit mind shuts down the physical mind and allows it to rest for awhile. We lose the sensation of feeling and thought. There is almost a complete cessation of conscious life.

"Somewhere in the spirit brain, like a programmed computer, body functions are controlled. When the spirit takes possession of the body before birth, the subconscious brain begins to control heartbeat, growth rate and other automatic functions. After birth, the spirit brain continues monitoring and controlling bodily activities, along with the major necessities of eating and sleeping. As we grow older, our physical mind begins to choose when we should sleep, but the spirit mind never sleeps. It continues on, controlling the body. If we sleep on one side too long, it sends a message to the physical brain and we roll over. If we begin to get cold, it regulates body temperature so we're warmer. It monitors the surrounding area for our protection, waking us at the slightest sound. If the heater or refrigerator goes on, it will say, 'All is well, sleep on.' Street noises, airplanes, railroads, anything we are familiar with will not wake us, but anything unfamiliar such as a door or window opening brings us wide awake.

"When we are awake the physical mind dominates and has several character properties the spirit mind lacks. The most important is reason, the ability to analyze and draw conclusions. Second is the God-given ability to choose, to act as a free agent. The spirit mind, with its temporary amnesia forced upon it from our pre-mortal life, is completely innocent and helpless if left to itself. It does not have the ability to choose or to reason, and this is an important fact to remember.

"As a great philosopher once said, 'I thinketh, therefore, I am.' Because of our ability to recall ideas and experiences, we are thinkers. We can check, weigh and evaluate what we hear or see, then decide whether or not we wish to believe it. Our physical mind is naturally suspicious. We tend to challenge things. We have the God-given power to discern between ideas. We refuse to believe anything unless we have a good reason. When we are hypnotized we lose these critical examining powers of the physical mind and our spirit mind accepts what the hypnotist says as fact. Once the hypnotist suggests something to our spirit mind, it carries out whatever function is demanded. The deeper the trance state, the more amazing the power released in the body when the subconscious accepts an idea from the hypnotist. Research labs report unusual demonstrations. After being hypnotized, students are told that their fingers were touched with a red-hot iron. Not only do their faces grimace with pain, but the lymph glands react as though actual contact had been made. Inflammation of the area and swelling will actually occur, even blisters appear. The spirit mind accepted the suggestion as fact.

"If, for some reason, the hypnotist desires you to forget whatever happened during the time you were under the spell, the experience, whether good or bad, would be completely blocked from your conscience.

"In a hypnotic suggestion, you are given a command that would influence your thinking after you awake. Thousands of smokers have gone to hypnotists to give up smoking. They are told that their cigarette will taste like burning rope. A strong influence from the subconscious convinces the conscious that the taste of tobacco smoke is really repulsive.

"In many night club acts, a subject called from the audience is told he is drunk. He may react as if dizzy and may even get sick. If he is told he is blind or lame, he will hobble pitifully around with his arms outstretched trying to find his way. If told he is sick, his body may develop a fever, weakness, sweating, even vomiting and convulsions. If told he is standing on hot coals, he will cry out in pain. If he is told to place his hands in a fire and not feel pain, his hands may be burnt. The feeling or sense of pain from the nervous system never gets past the spirit mind into the conscience, it is blocked. Reason, fear, judgement, all the protective characteristics of the conscious mind are numbed in sleep.

"There is a so-called rule that a hypnotized person cannot be forced to do anything against his moral standards. This is not true. It is a lie to deceive you and gain your confidence. Once under the spell of a unscrupulous hypnotist your spirit and body are completely lost to his demands. Hypnosis is dangerous. It has been found that the more a person is hypnotized, the easier it becomes to go under. At the snap of a finger or a single word, a subject can go into a hypnotic trance awaiting command.

"A very rich patient of an unscrupulous hypnotist, found himself compelled to give large gifts of money to the kind doctor. His wife and financial advisor questioned his generosity when he bought the hypnotherapist a Mercedes and donated a large sum of money to the doctor's private research fund.

"Another elderly man was confused when his children challenged his reason for changing his will, leaving everything to his doctor. He didn't know why he did it, and really didn't want to talk about it.

Copenhagen, Denmark, UPI, March 29, 1951 — "Palle Hardrupp, a 33 year old citizen of good moral upbringing, committed a bank robbery and shot to death the cashier and bank manager. Hardrupp had been hypnotized at least three times each week for three months by Bjorn Nielsen and told he must rob the bank and shoot the tellers if they refused to give him the money. Hardrupp, in committing the crime had acted contrary to his normal reasoning and desires. In a trance or semiconscious state, he fought the repeated hypnotic suggestive influence that nearly drove him into insanity.

"He had been driven, against popular beliefs, to criminal impulses by compulsion from without. Dr. Reiter, the psychiatrist, stated that any person can be capable of any act, and a hypnotist can ordinarily induce almost any person to commit a crime by repeatedly presenting the crime as having a worthy purpose. In this instance, Nielsen had persuaded Hardrupp that the ill-gotten money would be used to combat communism.

"Sixteen year old Cynthia was hypnotized along with ten other classmates at school, when another girl offered to demonstrate her newly acquired powers during an experiment on human behavior. The young hypnotist told the volunteers that they were freezing and all began to shake. The girl then told the ten that they were getting warmer and soon would wake up. Only Cynthia did not come out of the hypnotic state and continued to shake and began thrashing about crying, 'I'm freezing, I'm freezing!' The girl's parents were called and later said that apparently she recognized them, 'but she wouldn't, no matter how gentle we were, let us touch her.' She kept screaming, 'I'm cold, I'm cold, you're putting me in a freezer.' Cynthia was hospitalized and had a good night's sleep after being given sedatives." *(The Tulsa Tribune,* Oct. 7, 1970.)

"Dr. G. H. Estabrook of Cornell University, a psychologist and leading experimenter with hypnosis, particularly self-hypnosis, found himself able to conjure up an illusion. He hallucinated a polar bear and made a pet of it. To the learned Dr. Estabrook, his pet polar bear was just as real and as solid appearing as if it were actually alive and present. He was able to make the bear do anything he wanted it to do. On occasion he sent it padding around the hospital ward where he was a patient and once had it pat and kiss the nurses. It was a real source of amusement. However, after he was released from the hospital and no longer needed the imaginary bear to wile away the boring hours, it appeared anyway without being called. Sometimes, when he walked home from his classroom, the bear would join him for the stroll. The 'image' became so dominant that Dr. Estabrook awoke from a sound sleep one night and saw the polar bear sitting on the foot of his bed regarding him with interest. The professor finally put himself into a deep trance and banished the bear forever."

As a hypnotist, Betty Eadie would be able to use hypnosis to put a person, or group of people into an imaginary trance. She could also hypnotize herself into any number of imaginary dreams and fantasy excursions with make-believe characters. It is possible that Betty actually believes her delusions.

The author of *Overcoming Satan In The Latter Days*, Tim Wood, goes on to say:

"Imagination is one of the characteristics of the spirit mind. All new ideas, such as creativity and art, come from the spirit mind. It is the power of forming mental images of what is not present. Five artists, under hypnosis, were told that a coat rack was a tree. They all admired its beauty and said they would like to sketch it. They were provided with charcoal and paper. Each drawing was a masterpiece of art. Each drew a different tree, one Ash, another Walnut, a Pepper, an Oak and an Elm. Each artist saw a tree instead of a coat rack. The external forces of suggestion and control over the spirit mind and power of imagination was greatly expressed in this experiment.

"In the following example, several subjects were told they could see a monster. As their imagination began to run wild, they reacted in stark terror. Asked to draw the creatures they saw, they drew pictures that were comparable to those mental patients had drawn after fits of hallucination.

"If through the power of suggestion or hypnotism, influences on the spirit mind can bring such imaginations and illustrations as these, think what havoc Satan's influence can have. If false spirits can deceive people into giving themselves over to evil influences, they can easily suggest ideas into the conscious mind, controlling the imagination of the subconscious, or spirit mind. It makes sense to understand how easily you can be forced to hallucinate polar bears, serpents, dragons and demons.

"President Francis M. Lyman of the Council of the Twelve wrote: 'From what I understand and have seen, I should advise you not to practice hypnotism. For my own part I could never consent to being or allowing one of my children to be. The free agency that the Lord has given us is the choicest gift we have. As soon, however, as we permit another mind to control us, as that mind controls its own body and functions, we have completely surrendered our free agency to another; and so long as we are in the hypnotic spell, and that is as long as the hypnotist desires us to be, we give no consent in any sense whatever to anything we do. The hypnotist might influence us to do good things, but we could receive no benefit from that, even if we remember it after coming out of the spell, for it was not done voluntarily. The hypnotist might also influence us to do absurd and even shocking, wicked things, for his will compels us.' *(Era,* Vol. 6, pg. 420.)

"Brigham Young voiced the same sentiments: 'The principles of hypnotism are true, but wicked men use it to an evil purpose, to promote the causes of the devil.' *(JD 6:370.)*

"There is similarity between the hypnotized and the possessed. Those hypnotized are controlled by the hypnotist, those possessed are controlled by devils in the same manner through the subconscious. Thus compulsion is like a hypnotic suggestion to the subconscious, it takes over the body, fulfilling the commands of the devils." (Wood, Timothy. *"Overcoming Satan in the Latter Days,"* 1987. pgs. 257-263, 265-266.)

Betty Eadie and the Eadie-ites must prayerfully examine the seriousness of their wayward position in relationship to the teachings of the Savior regarding "hypnotism" and the true requirement for entrance into the kingdom of God. Elder Bernard P. Brockbank taught that, "We all have the responsibility of preparing ourselves and others for entrance back into the kingdom of God.

"The atoning sacrifice of Jesus Christ made it possible for all mankind to be resurrected and to be raised to immortality. These are universal gifts from God.

"The Apostle Paul taught: 'For as in Adam all die, even so in Christ shall all be made alive.' *(1 Cor. 15:22.)*

"But to be resurrected and immortal is not all that is required for entrance into eternal life in the kingdom of God. Eternal life in the kingdom of God is far beyond His universal gift of immortality and is God's greatest gift to all mankind; it can only be brought about through obedience to the doctrines and commandments taught by Jesus Christ.

"Jesus said, 'I am the way, the truth and the life; no man cometh unto the father, but by Me.' *(John 14:6.)* He said, '. . . no man cometh unto the Father, but by Me.' This is the Lord's way, and coming unto the Father is a divine and sacred gift that must be merited.

"Again, Jesus Christ said, '. . . Trifle not with sacred things. If thou wilt do good, yea, and hold out faithful to the end, thou shalt be saved in the kingdom of God, which is the greatest of all of the gifts of God, for there is no gift greater than the gift of salvation.' *(D&C 6:12-13.)* God's greatest gift and blessing to His children is eternal life with Him in His heavenly kingdom.

"Today there is much controversy and contention among the doctrines and philosophies of men relative to the requirements for entrance into the kingdom of God. Many have been deceived by the teachings of men that works and obedience to God's commandments are not essential, and some base their contention on scriptures. For example, Paul said, 'For by grace are ye saved through faith; and that not of yourselves: it is the gift of God: Not of works, lest any man should boast.' *(Eph. 2:8-9.)*

"The resurrection and immortality are gifts from God, through Jesus Christ, and not from the works and efforts of mortal men.

"Many try to justify their claims with the statement of Jesus to the thief, when the thief said to Jesus, 'Lord, remember me when thou comest into thy kingdom,' and Jesus said unto him, 'Verily I say unto thee, To day shalt thou be with Me in paradise.' *(Luke 23:42-43.)* Jesus and the thief went to paradise. There are those who teach that paradise and heaven are one and the same place, but this is not according to the teachings of the holy scriptures.

"After mortal death the spirit goes to paradise and remains there until the appointed time for its resurrection into immortality and eternal life.

"Heaven, which is the kingdom of God, is where those who have been obedient to God's plan of life and salvation go after judgment and the resurrection.

"The spirit of Jesus, after His death, went to paradise and not to the kingdom of heaven. It was not until after His resurrection that He mentioned returning to the kingdom of heaven. You will recall His words to Mary as she stood by the sepulcher weeping: 'Touch me not, for I am not yet ascended to My Father: But go to My brethren, and say unto them;, I ascend unto My Father, and your Father; and to My God, and your God.' *(John 20:17.)* His spirit had been to paradise, but He had not yet ascended to His Father in heaven.

"Jesus warned that not very many would find their way and prepare themselves to live in the kingdom of heaven. He said, 'Enter ye in at the strait gate: . . . Because strait is the gate, and narrow is the way, which leadeth unto life, and few there be that find it.' *(Matt. 7:13-14.)*

"Many, according to Jesus will be misled and deceived by false teachers and false prophets, and some will desire to follow the ways of the world and will destroy their divine opportunity to enter into the kingdom of heaven. He said, '. . . wide is the gate, and broad is the way, that leadeth to destruction, and many there be which go in thereat.' *(Matt. 7:13.)*

"Contrary to what many think, just believing in God and being virtuous and pure are not sufficient to qualify a person for entrance into the kingdom of heaven. The Savior's parable about the ten virgins and their desire to enter the kingdom of heaven makes this point very clear. Jesus said:

"Then shall the kingdom of heaven be likened unto ten virgins, which took their lamps, and went forth to meet the bridegroom.

'And five of them were wise, and five were foolish.

'They that were foolish took their lamps.

'While the bridegroom tarried, they all slumbered and slept.

'And at midnight there was a cry made, Behold, the bridegroom cometh; go ye out to meet Him.

'Then all those virgins arose, and trimmed their lamps.

'And the foolish said unto the wise, Give us of your oil; for our lamps are gone out.

'But the wise answered, saying, "Not so; lest there be not enough for us and you: but go ye rather to them that sell, and buy for yourselves."

'And while they went to buy, the bridegroom came; and they that were ready went in with Him to the marriage: and the door was shut.

'Afterward came also the other virgins, saying, "Lord, Lord, open to us."

'But He answered and said, "Verily I say unto you, I know you not." *(Matt. 25:1-12.)*

"Take note that the Lord was not talking about five thieves and sinners and five good people; he was talking about ten virgins, ten pure people who believed in God and had a desire to enter into the kingdom of heaven. The five foolish virgins had failed to prepare. Their lights were out; they were in darkness. Their urgent pleas and hasty preparation were not sufficient, and they heard these words from the lips of their God: 'I know you not.'

"What a shame to be clean and yet unprepared! What a tragedy to fail in service to God and in helping to build His kingdom on earth as it is in heaven! What a shame to be in darkness when the light of Christ has been made possible for everyone!

"Jesus, speaking of good people who failed to qualify for entrance into the kingdom of heaven, said, 'These are they who are not valiant in the testimony of Jesus; wherefore, they obtain not the crown over the kingdom of our God.' *(D&C 76:79.)*

"It is a divine warning from the teachings of Jesus Christ that one must be prepared to enter into the kingdom of heaven and must have the light of life that is made possible through following Jesus Christ. Jesus said, 'I am the light of the world: He that followeth Me shall not walk in darkness, but shall have the light of life.' *(John 8:12.)*

"The light of life can come only through following Jesus Christ. The light of life is divine light and is required in the immortal soul before entrance back into the kingdom of God. You cannot obtain the divine light of life from men. It does not come from just being good. It can only come through repentance and by living the gospel plan of life and salvation as given by Jesus Christ.

"When Jesus lived on the earth, He found a very religious group of people known as the Pharisees. They believed in God; they accepted the teaching of the prophets in the Old Testament. They accepted the Ten Commandments and would not even pick up a stone on the Sabbath day in their compliance with the commandment relative to keeping the Sabbath day holy. Yet Jesus said of the devout, praying Pharisees:

'This people draweth nigh unto Me with their mouth, and honoureth Me with their lips; but their heart is far from Me.

'But in vain they do worship Me, teaching for doctrines the commandments of men.' *(Matt. 15:8-9.)*

"They had changed the Lord's commandments into commandments of men.

"In His Sermon on the Mount Jesus Christ also mentioned to these people their qualification for entering into the kingdom of heaven through the Pharisee religion, with its man-made doctrines and commandments. He said, 'For I say unto you, That except your righteousness shall exceed the righteousness of the scribes and Pharisees, ye shall in no case enter into the kingdom of heaven.' *(Matt. 5:20.)*

"The Pharisees, in all of their dedication and their love for God and the ancient prophets and their obedience to man-made righteousness, which appeared to be taken from the scriptures, did not qualify for entrance into the kingdom of heaven. The Pharisees were worshipping a mystical god of spirit, and they were unable to know the living God when He appeared before them. He tried with all of His godly power to convince them, but they would rather defend their man-made church and their man-made doctrines than accept the church and teachings of Jesus Christ.

"All men should know what acts will keep them from entering the kingdom of heaven. According to the Apostle Paul, the following works of the flesh will keep a person out of the kingdom of God: '. . . Adultery, fornication, uncleanness, lasciviousness, idolatry, witchcraft, hatred, variance, emulations, wrath, strife, seditions, heresies, envyings, murders, drunkenness, revelings, and such life: . . . they which do such things shall not inherit the kingdom of God.' *(Gal. 5:19-21.)*

"Indulgence in works of the flesh will destroy man's divine nature and potential godliness.

"Repentance makes it possible to cleanse the mind and body, of these sins, except murder, and all other weaknesses, and to turn to the Lord's way of life. He said, 'Repent, for the kingdom of heaven is at hand.' *(Matt. 4:17.)*

"Repentance is God's way, with the help of His doctrines and commandments, to purify and cleanse the mind and body of its weaknesses and imperfections.

"Repentance frees the conscience and cleanses the mind. Jesus said, 'Behold, he who has repented of his sins, the same is forgiven, and I, the Lord, remember them no more. By this ye may know if a man repenteth of his sins—behold, he will confess them and forsake them.' *(D&C 58:42-43.)*

"Repentance prepares the mind and body to know the living God and the living Jesus Christ and to receive the gospel and take on the divine light of life.

"It is important to know that all of the requirements for entrance into the kingdom of God were personally given by Jesus Christ and are recorded in His holy scriptures. There will be many good people turned away from entrance into the kingdom of heaven because they failed to know and follow the Lord's plan of life. They were more interested in following doctrines of men and commandments of men than they were in following the doctrines of the Lord, as recorded in His scriptures. They were more interested in defending their sect or denomination than in knowing the truth.

"Here are some of the keys that Jesus Christ gave to help one qualify for entrance back into the kingdom of God.

"Jesus said, 'Verily, verily, I say unto thee, Except a man be born again, he cannot see the kingdom of God' *(John 3:3)*; 'Except a man be born of water and of the Spirit, he cannot enter into the kingdom of God' *(John 3:5.)*

In John 17, verse 3, another key is recorded by Jesus Christ: ". . . this is life eternal, that they might know thee the only true God, and Jesus Christ, whom thou has sent.'

"Wouldn't you think it is important to know God the Eternal Father and Jesus Christ if you expect to live with them in the kingdom of heaven? Many feel that they know God and know Jesus Christ, but they fail to keep their commandments.

"Hear the words of the Apostle John to all who claim to know God. He said, 'And hereby we do know that we know

Him, if we keep His commandments. He that saith, I know Him, and keepeth not His commandments, is a liar, and the truth is not in him.' *(1 John 2:3-4.)*

"Knowing God is shown by keeping His commandments. People who accept and live doctrines of men do not know the living God. When you know the living God and the living Christ, you will also know your divine relationship to God.

"Jesus asked us to pray to our Father in heaven and to 'seek ye first the kingdom of God, and His righteousness.'" *(Matt. 6:33.)*

(Bernard P. Brockbank, *Passage to Light*, 1979, pgs. 115-123.)

Chapter Five

Which Church Is Right?

Betty Eadie and Curtis Taylor are both baptized, active members of The Church of Jesus Christ of Latter-day Saints. Both have been through the temple and have been active participants in the Mormon Church for many, many years. If you read the last paragraph on page 45 of *Embraced by the Light*, you will be shocked that Curtis and Betty could be so bold as to print that: "NO ONE CHURCH CAN FULFILL EVERYBODY'S NEEDS AT EVERY LEVEL." It is unbelievable that members of the Lord's true and restored church could dare make such a damning statement. Did they lose their faith in Christ and belief in His church? No one knows. Remember, the Mormon Church embodies the fullness of the gospel of Jesus Christ.

Eadie and Taylor continue to compound their blasphemy by publishing on page 46 that Betty "knew that we have no right to criticize any church or religion in any way. They are all precious and important in His sight." This is a lie; a serious error which must be corrected immediately!

Joseph Smith received completely opposite information from our Father in heaven and from Jesus Christ than that which Betty claims to have received. Who is telling the truth,

Joseph Smith the prophet . . . or Betty Eadie? Let's read the
Prophet Joseph Smith's testimony as told to us in his own
words: "I was born in the year of our Lord one thousand eight
hundred and five, on the twenty-third day of December, in the
town of Sharon, Windsor county, state of Vermont, and moved
to Palmyra, Ontario (now Wayne) county, in the state of New
York, when I was in my tenth year, or thereabouts. In about
four years after my father's arrival in Palmyra he moved with
his family into Manchester, in the same county of Ontario.

"Some time in the second year after our removal to
Manchester, there was in the place where we lived an unusual
excitement on the subject of religion. It commenced with the
Methodists, but soon became general among all the sects in
that region. Indeed, the whole district seemed affected by it,
and great multitudes united themselves to the different
religious parties, which created no small stir and division
amongst the people, some crying, 'Lo, here!' and others, 'Lo,
there!' Some were contending for the Methodist faith, some for
the Presbyterian, and some for the Baptist.

"For notwithstanding the great love which the converts to
these different faiths expressed at the time of their conversion,
and the great zeal manifested by the respective clergy, who
were active in getting up and promoting this extraordinary
scene of religious feeling, in order to have everybody
converted, as they were pleased to call it, let them join what
sect they pleased—yet when the converts began to file off, some
to one party and some to another, it was seen that the
seemingly good feelings of both the priests and converts were
more pretended than real; for a scene of great confusion and
bad feeling ensued; priest contending against priest, and
convert against convert; so that all their good feelings one for
another, if they ever had any, were entirely lost in a strife of
words and contest about opinions.

"I was at this time in my fifteenth year. My father's family was proselyted to the Presbyterian faith, and four of them joined that church, namely—my mother, Lucy; my brothers Hyrum and Samuel Harrison; and my sister Sophronia.

"During this time of great excitement, my mind was called up to serious reflection and great uneasiness; but, though my feelings were deep and often poignant, still I kept myself aloof from all these parties, though I attended their several meetings as often as occasion would permit. In process of time my mind became somewhat partial to the Methodist sect, and I felt some desire to be united with them; but so great were the confusion and strife among the different denominations, that it was impossible for a person young as I was and so unacquainted with men and things, to come to any certain conclusion who was right and who was wrong.

"My mind at times was greatly excited, the cry and tumult were so great and incessant.

"In the midst of this war of words and tumult of opinions, I often said to myself, 'What is to be done? Who of all these parties are right; or, are they all wrong together? If any one of them be right, which is it, and how shall I know it?'

"While I was laboring under the extreme difficulties caused by the contests of these parties of religionists, I was one day reading the Epistle of James, first chapter and fifth verse, which reads: *'If any of you lack wisdom, let him ask of God, that giveth to all men liberally, and upbraideth not; and it shall be given him.'*

"Never did any passage of scripture come with more power to the heart of man than this did at this time to mine. It seemed to enter with great force into every feeling of heart. I reflected on it again and again, knowing that if any person needed wisdom from God, I did; for how to act I did not know, and unless I could get more wisdom that I then had, I would never know; for the teachers of religion of the different sects understood the same passage of scripture so differently as to destroy all confidence in settling the question by an appeal to the Bible.

"At length I came to the conclusion that I must either remain in darkness and confusion, or else I must do as James directs, that is, ask of God. I at length came to the determination to 'ask of God,' concluding that if He gave wisdom to them that lacked wisdom and would give liberally, and not upbraid, I might venture.

"So, in accordance with this, my determination to ask of God, I retired to the woods to make the attempt. It was on the morning of a beautiful, clear day, early in the spring of eighteen hundred and twenty. It was the first time in my life that I had made such an attempt, for amidst all my anxieties I had never as yet made the attempt to pray vocally.

"After I had retired to the place were I had previously designed to go, having looked around me, and finding myself alone, I kneeled down and began to offer up the desires of my heart to God. I had scarcely done so, when immediately I was seized upon by some power which entirely overcame me, and had such an astonishing influence over me as to bind my tongue so that I could not speak. Thick darkness gathered around me, and it seemed to me for a time as if I were doomed to sudden destruction.

"But, exerting all my powers to call upon God to deliver me out of the power of this enemy which had seized upon me, and at the very moment when I was ready to sink into despair and abandon myself to destruction—not to an imaginary ruin, but to the power of some actual being from an unseen world, who had such marvelous power as I had never before felt in any being—just at this moment of great alarm, I saw a pillar of light exactly over my head, above the brightness of the sun, which descended gradually until it fell upon me.

"It no sooner appeared than I found myself delivered from the enemy which held me bound. When the light rested upon me I saw two Personages, whose brightness and glory defy all description, standing above me in the air. One of them spake unto me, calling me by name, and said—pointing to the other—'This is my Beloved Son, Hear Him!'

"My object in going to inquire of the Lord was to know which of all the sects was right, that I might know which to join. No sooner, therefore, did I get possession of myself, so as to be able to speak, than I asked the Personages who stood above me in the light, which of all the sects was right—and which I should join.

"I was answered that I must join none of them, for they were all wrong, and the Personage who addressed me said that their creeds were an abomination in His sight; that those professors were all corrupt; that 'they draw near unto Me with their lips, but their hearts are far from Me; they teach for doctrines the commandments of men: having a form of godliness, but they deny the power thereof.'

"He again forbade me to join with any of them; and many other things He did say unto me, which I cannot write at this time. When I came to myself again, I found myself lying on my back, looking up into heaven.

"Some few days after I had this vision, I happened to be in company with one of the Methodist preachers, who was very active in the before-mentioned religious excitement; and, conversing with him on the subject of religion, I took occasion to give him an account of the vision which I had. I was greatly surprised at his behavior; he treated my communication not only lightly, but with great contempt, saying, it was all of the devil, that there were no such things as visions or revelations in these days; that all such things had ceased with the apostles, and that there would never be any more of them.

"I soon found, however, that my telling the story had excited a great deal of prejudice against me amongst professors of religion, and was the cause of a great persecution, which continued to increase; and though I was an obscure boy, only between fourteen and fifteen years of age, and my circumstances in life such as to make a boy of no consequence in the world, yet men of high standing would take notice sufficient to excite the public mind against me; and create a bitter persecution; and this was common among all the sects—all united to persecute me.

"It caused me serious reflection then, and often has since, how very strange it was that an obscure boy, of a little over fourteen years of age, and one, too, who was doomed to the necessity of obtaining a scanty maintenance by his daily labor, should be thought a character of sufficient importance to attract the attention of the great ones of the most popular sects of the day, and in a manner to create in them a spirit of the most bitter persecution and reviling. But strange or not, so it was, and it was often the cause of great sorrow to myself.

"However, it was nevertheless a fact that I had beheld a vision. I have thought since, that I felt much like Paul, when he made his defense before King Agrippa, and related the account of the vision he had when he saw a light, and heard a voice; but still there were but few who believed him; some said he was dishonest, others said he was mad; and he was ridiculed and reviled. But all this did not destroy the reality of his vision. He had seen a vision, he knew he had, and all the persecution under heaven could not make it otherwise; and though they should persecute him unto death, yet he knew, and would know to his latest breath, that he had both seen a light and heard a voice speaking unto him, and all the world could not make him think or believe otherwise.

"So it was with me. I had actually seen a light, and in the midst of that light I saw two Personages, and they did in reality speak to me; and though I was hated and persecuted for saying that I had seen a vision, yet it was true; and while they were persecuting me, reviling me, and speaking all manner of evil against me falsely for so saying, I was led to say in my heart: Why persecute me for telling the truth? I have actually seen a vision; and who am I that I can withstand God, or why does the world think to make me deny what I have actually seen? For I had seen a vision; I knew it, and I knew that God knew it, and I could not deny it, neither dared I do it; at least I knew that by so doing I would offend God, and come under condemnation.

"I had now got my mind satisfied so far as the sectarian world was concerned—that it was not my duty to join with any of them, but to continue as I was until further directed. I had found the testimony of James to be true—that a man who lacked wisdom might ask of God, and obtain, and not be upbraided." *(JS 1:3-26.)*

Is there any question who is telling the truth? Joseph Smith received a personal visitation in answer to his sincere prayers to God. Betty Eadie says many times that "the heavens scrolled back" *(Embraced, pgs. 98, 103, 121)* and Jesus showed her visions that no other prophet since Adam has ever witnessed . . . and all this occurred as she was being embraced by the Savior. Who do you believe is telling the truth? When measured against the scriptural standards, the answer is clear. When fasting and prayer is involved, the answer becomes more clear. Those who profess to be "Eadie-ites" and believers in Betty's brand of Christianity need to seriously evaluate the dangerous ground they walk upon.

In 1994 when Betty Eadie appeared on the Oprah Winfrey television show, she was viewed in 8.6 million households. Television marketing and research professionals say that 2.5 people in each home viewed the show. Two and a half viewers in approximately 8,600,000 homes means that over 21 1/2 million people, that's 21,500,000 television viewers watched Betty Eadie and Oprah Winfrey. It is also important to remember that the show has been replayed on Oprah reruns. The importance of these sizeable numbers is that over 40 million (40,000,000) curious and often vulnerable people have viewed and heard Betty J. Eadie falsely proclaim that she "spoke with" and was "embraced by" our Savior . . . and had a personal "guided tour" of the heavens!

Oprah Winfrey asked Betty if the personage in the light at the end of the death tunnel was Jesus Christ. Betty responded by saying, "He didn't say He was Jesus Christ, but I knew who He was." Eadie's book says quite the opposite. Mrs. Eadie also said, "That it could be the religious leader of whatever religion the person believes in that greets them." Betty jokingly told Oprah that her husband, Joe Eadie, thought she had "lost her marbles." Betty admitted to the millions of television viewers, and the studio audience, that what she claims "sounds crazy" but that she "doesn't care that it sounds crazy." Oprah asked Betty, on the show, if "she was lying and scamming us?" Betty has probably related this hypothetical experience so may times she now probably believes that her visit with the Lord actually occurred! If Betty would have admitted that it was just a dream, or if she would have said, "It would be marvelous if this could really happen" then it would not be so damaging. How many of the 40 million viewers really believed what Betty was saying? How many naive children of God now believe that it really doesn't matter what church a person belongs to . . . or that a person must accomplish specific goals as taught by Christ to enter back into His presence? The false information and eternal damage could be greater and more far-reaching than any of us realize!

Betty Eadie also told Oprah Winfrey and her millions that, "she learned from Jesus that we judge ourselves" in the hereafter. This is blasphemy to all Christians! It is totally untrue and must be corrected by Betty Eadie and Curtis Taylor immediately. The scriptures are replete with references that "we shall all stand before the judgement seat of Christ." *(Romans 14:10.)* The unrighteous want to believe Betty.

Embraced by the Light has been on the New York Times and Publishers Weekly bestsellers lists for over a year. The audio cassette version of the "Embraced" book which is personally read onto tape by Betty Eadie is also one of Publishers Weekly and Ingram's top ten bestsellers. Ironically, *Embraced by the Light* appears on the non-fiction side of these particular lists . . . when in fact it should appear on the fiction lists because what Betty writes about did not really happen at all! Her visit with Christ was fiction!

Betty was forced to drop out of high school when she was 15 years old. She married at age 15, and later divorced at age 21, after bearing 4 children. *("Embraced," pgs. 15-16.)* Without the aid and assistance of her "ghost writers," Betty's first novel, *Embraced by the Light* would have never seen the inside of a bookstore.

Chapter Six

No Unclean Thing Can Enter

"**B**ut behold, I say unto you, the kingdom of God is not filthy, and there cannot any unclean thing enter into the kingdom of God . . ." *(1 Nephi 15:34.)*

Was Betty selected for this "celestial grand tour" over and above all the other innocent and righteous spirits who died at the same time Betty claims to have died? Was she chosen by the Savior because of her innocence, purity and cleanliness? Remember that no unclean thing can enter into the presence of God. In Moses 6:7 we read: "Wherefore teach it unto your children, that all men, everywhere, must repent, or they can in nowise inherit the kingdom of God, for no unclean thing can dwell there, or dwell in His presence . . ." The Prophet Nephi stated that: "in heaven, . . . nothing doth corrupt, and . . . nothing can come which is unclean . . ." *(Helaman 8:25.)* A very important revelation given by the Lord to the Prophet Joseph Smith at Kirtland, Ohio, May 6, 1883 says: "And ye shall not suffer any unclean thing to come in unto it; and My glory shall be there; and My presence shall be there. But if there shall come into it any unclean thing, My glory shall not be there; and My presence shall not come into it." *(D&C 94: 8-9.)*

Our Lord and Savior Jesus Christ also instructed His disciples and members of the church by declaring these qualifications for entrance into God's presence: "And no unclean thing can enter into His kingdom; therefore nothing entereth into His rest save it be those who have washed their garments in My blood, because of their faith, and the repentance of all their sins, and their faithfulness unto the end." *(3 Nephi 27:10.)* Betty Eadie admits that she was not flawless, and that she is not flawless even today. Moses could not touch God as Betty claims to have done. No other prophet or apostle in history has ever been able to "embrace the Savior" as Betty claims to have done. It takes a millennium of repentance and perfection to be able to fully qualify one's self to even be in His presence, let alone, touch His robes and embrace. Betty admits in the book, *Embraced by the Light* that she was not qualified. It makes no sense and is scripturally unsound and erroneous.

Can Betty set herself up as high or higher than the prophets and apostles of old, and those of today? Was she more innocent, clean and pure in heart? Was she ordained with the Priesthood of God? She says no! Betty claims she was told to return to earth and complete her mission, but says she doesn't know what that mission is. God is not the author of confusion. Nor would Jesus send someone on a mission without letting them understand what that mission is. All people's of the earth were sent here on a specific mission, and through the scriptures, revelation and prayer, each of us can fully discover and understand the mission we are to fulfill.

Embraced by the Light violates the revealed word of God and the Holy Scriptures and makes a mockery of all eternal truth. It confuses the beliefs and proper goals of all true members of Christ's church. If it is contrary to the revealed word of God, then it is a lie! Is Betty's "divine mission" to mislead and confuse the world as to what really and truly happens to the soul and spirit after death? No! God's house is a house of order, not a "house of confusion and fantasy," pretend and make-believe. If Betty returned to earth to fulfill a "mission" directive of the Savior as she claims, wouldn't it make sense that she would not only remember her instructions but that she would immediately begin her mission and not waste 2 decades (almost 20 years) for someone to write it for her? Why the wait if it actually happened?

A vision of the celestial sphere would be difficult, if not impossible, to describe. That was the dilemma of the prophet Isaiah. He endeavored to portray something of the power and glory of his experience, using images and terms with which his readers could identify (see Isaiah Chap. 6.) Even then, Isaiah sensed how much he fell short of communicating the reality of the experience. Later in his writing, Isaiah described the inadequacy of words and even of the senses of mortal man to comprehend heavenly things. He wrote: "For since the beginning of the world men have not heard, nor perceived by the ear, neither hath the eye seen, O God, beside thee, what He hath prepared for him that waiteth for Him" *(Isaiah 64:4.)*

The Apostle Paul also instructed the members and saints of the early church when he cited Isaiah by saying: "But it is written, Eye hath not seen, nor ear heard, neither have entered into the heart of man, the things which God hath prepared for them that love Him." *(1 Corinthians 2:9.)* Betty Eadie did not see, nor did she hear, nor did the wondrous secrets of the hereafter enter into her heart.

The Prophet Joseph Smith further illuminated and provided a perspective on the life hereafter when he said: "Could we read and comprehend all that has been written from the days of Adam, on the relation of man to God and angels in a future state, we should know very little about it. Knowledge of these things can only be obtained by experience through the ordinances of God set forth for that purpose. Could you gaze into heaven five minutes, you would know more than you would by reading all that ever was written on the subject." *(Teachings,* pg. 324.)

Embraced by the Light reached popularity and peaked in 1994 as a direct result of the increasing age of the "baby-boomer" generation now in their 40's and 50's. An age group which, in large numbers worldwide, distanced itself from God and religion in the past, and are now longing for answers to important questions about life after death. The real truth must be shown and taught to them. There is no room for personal fantasy and make-believe as a false substitute for the revealed truth of God. The truth should be proclaimed and all of the children of our Father in heaven must be accurately informed as to the glorious life after death.

When Betty Eadie and Gold Leaf Press began their media blitz to promote their *Embraced by the Light* collaboration, they hired an advertising and public relations agency by the name of Hal Gardiner and Associates in Salt Lake City. This public relations ad agency distributed free books and information to hundreds of newspapers and bookstores. One of Hal Gardiner's agency associates by the name of Elese Adams drafted a cover letter which boasted the 1992 sales figures for the "Embraced" book.

One newspaper editor who received his complimentary copy and free information was John Heinerman of the Utah Senior Prime Times. In March of 1993 Editor Heinerman wrote and published in his newspaper that: "Betty J. Eadie, the author, is of Sioux-LDS (Mormon) background. Whether or not she actually died and went into the netherworld remains to be seen. But, at the very least, she spins a darned good tale. The dialogue is a bit wooden and stiff in places, but she manages to persuade her readers that something happened to her on that particular day (November 18, 1973) in the hospital."

Mr. Heinerman continues: "After having left her body (so she says), '. . . I saw a pinpoint of light in the distance . . . As I approached it, I noticed the figure of a man standing in it, with light radiating all around him.'" (*Embraced by the Light, pg. 40.*) The editor goes on to describe, "What follows next is a sort of non-sexual intimacy in which masculine and feminine light energies presumably 'merged together' in a weird kind of cosmic intercourse."

Quoting directly from page 41 of Betty's book, it reads, "I felt His light blending into mine, literally, and I felt my light being drawn to His. It was as if there were two lamps in a room, both shining, their light merging together. It's hard to tell where one light ends and the other begins; they just become one light. And as our lights merged . . . I felt an utter explosion of love."

John Heinerman further writes that these statements of Betty's, "suggest an ethereal kind of love-making without the physical benefits of the flesh. This orgiastic event of the soul was undoubtedly an emotional high for Ms. Eadie. She has succeeded in doing probably what no other writer of romance novels or sexual potboilers has ever done. And that is to describe a form of "spiritual sexuality" in which the obvious lusts of passion expressed are more transcendental in their makeup than actually bonafide in the true physical sense."

The Utah Senior Times critiques *Embraced by the Light* stating: "If you like light, breezy, almost escapism type of reading then this book is sure to please you. On the other hand, if you prefer your facts about the hereafter in a more convincing fashion, then this work will surely disappoint you." After Betty failed to show up for an interview scheduled by

Hal Gardiner and Associates and their representative Elese Adams, the newspaper writes: "Seeing as how Ms. Eadie is part Native American, she should worry less about "The Light" and concern herself more with keeping her own appointments. After all, for a woman in her position presumably espousing "truths" about the next life, it doesn't look very good for this half-Indian to be speaking with a forked tongue." *(Utah Senior Prime Times,* March 1993, page 20-21.)

Those who enter into the Kingdom of God after being judged clean, repentant and worthy to do so may become angels of the Most High. The Prophet Joseph Smith said that: "The spirits of the just are exalted to a greater and more glorious work; hence they are blessed in their departure to the world of spirits. Enveloped in flaming fire, they are not far from us, and know and understand our thoughts, feelings, and emotions, and are often pained therewith."

Heber C. Kimball spoke very eloquently about the angels of the Lord when he said: "Who are His angels? They are men who stood fast through tribulation; they are prophets and apostles and patriarchs who once lived upon the earth, and bore testimony of the truth of the Gospel of the Son of God, the same Gospel that we preach. If we try to gather the poor, the Lord and His angels will help us and open the way before us.

"My prayer is that our hearts may become full with the word of God and with the power of God, showing our connection with God, with Jesus Christ, and with the Holy Ghost, with the angels, and with the prophets and apostles that dwell in heaven.

"I will make another remark regarding angels. God sent an angel to John on the Isle of Patmos, and John says, concerning it, 'and I fell at His feet to worship Him. And He said unto me, see though do it not; I am thy fellow servant, and of thy brethren that have the testimony of Jesus—worship God.' Men are made a little lower than the angels for the suffering of death, but when men are clothed with the holy priesthood and sent forth to minister the word of life, the comparison between them and the angels is somewhat different. 'And of His angels He saith, Who maketh His angels spirits, and His ministers a flame of fire.' While in the act of ministering the Gospel, the servants of God may be considered angels. 'Be not forgetful to entertain strangers, for some have entertained angels unawares.' The servants of God are angels in one sense, sent forth to gather the house of Israel from the four corners of the earth.

"The Lord sent three angels to watch over Abraham and Lot anciently. They stayed with Abraham, and Sarah baked a cake a piece for them; Abraham killed a calf, and supplied butter and milk to refresh them, after they had washed their feet. Jacob, on one occasion, wrestled with an angel all night long, but could not throw him. Jacob had hold of a being full of spring and power like unto a man, and he did not know the difference; he was a man and an angel. We are exhorted daily to conduct ourselves like the angels of God, to try and be like them." *(Journal of Discourses* 10:102-103.)

Betty's alleged death and her subsequent resurrection in November of 1973 was not her first death experience. She says on page 4 and 5 of her book that she was pronounced dead at the age of 4 years old. The doctor diagnosed the illness as "double-pneumonia" and "whooping cough" and the accompanying fever is what brought on Betty's first death.

Even though the hospital staff had pulled the covers up over her head and said, "We've lost her," Betty was able to look around the hospital room, and to her amazement she was able to do so "even though the covers were pulled over my face" she said. Betty claims to have been "picked up, held and cradled and gently rocked" by a heavenly being when she died at the age of 4 years. An amazing memory for a 4 year old with double pneumonia, whooping cough and a deadly fever. It's an amazing story about a deathly ill little girl who "giggled and ran her hands through the beard (of the heavenly being) and twirled it on my fingers" or so Betty claims. Whether this celestial being was supposed to be God the Father or Jesus Christ is not known by Betty, but the fact that she claims to have been touched by Him is contrary to the word of God. She claims to have touched His personage and "felt calm and happy with him." *(Embraced, pg. 5.)*

What Betty Eadie describes about her two deaths and her two subsequent resurrections at age 4 and age 31 are very suspect. The Prophet Alma told his son Corianton: "But whether it be at His resurrection or after, I do not say; but this much I say, that there is a space between death and the resurrection of the body, and a state of the soul in happiness or in misery until the time which is appointed of God that the dead shall come forth, and be reunited, both soul and body, and be brought to stand before God, and be judged according to their works." *(Alma 40:21.)*

We must keep in mind the statement of President Joseph F. Smith, Anthon H. Lund, and Charles W. Penrose (then the First Presidency) as they admonish: "When visions, dreams, tongues, prophecy, impressions or any extraordinary gift of inspiration convey something out of harmony with the accepted revelations of the Church or contrary to the decisions of its constituted authorities, Latter-day Saints may know that it is not of God, no matter how plausible it may appear." *(Messages of the First Presidency, 4:285.)* Betty's book is "out of harmony."

The store managers of the Deseret Book stores which are operated by The Church of Jesus Christ of Latter-day Saints were instructed to place the book, *Embraced by the Light* in the fiction section of the bookstore because it did not comply with scriptural doctrine . . . and Betty's book is fiction.

When Betty Eadie traveled the state of Utah and filled school gymnasiums with curious spectators she refused to answer questions from the audience for fear that she would be quizzed as to the truthfulness of the incidents proclaimed in her book. Many of the organizers of these local events were paid for their assistance, marketing and promotional efforts with free copies of Betty's book *Embraced by the Light*. Mormon Church members were found standing in monthly fast and testimony meetings bearing testimony to the truthfulness of the "Embraced" book! They were not testifying about the *Book of Mormon* or the Bible, but to their "false enlightenment" of Betty Eadie's book! The Mormon Church's educational system headquartered in Salt Lake City discovered that some of their Seminary teachers were actually referring to Betty's book when they instructed their naive students. A letter demanding that these teachers cease and desist this practice was delivered to all of the seminary staff churchwide. Much to the amazement of many Latter-day Saints was that the contents of the "Embraced" book were even being taught in Relief Society, Sunday School and Priesthood meetings by those lacking sufficient knowledge of scriptural doctrine to see the inconsistencies with church teachings.

Those who attended some of the "traveling roadshows" where Betty told her life after death story, were led to believe that these nightly meetings were sponsored by the Mormon Church. The initial onslaught of book sales were generated by purchases made by members of The Church of Jesus Christ of Latter-day Saints. *The Book of Mormon* should be so popular and sought-after.

Chapter Seven

Do Sins Really Matter?

One of the most seriously misleading and erroneous teachings which Betty Eadie says she received directly from the Lord is found in various sections of her book, *Embraced by the Light*. She begins on page 41 of the book by stating: ". . . as I saw his (the Lord's) arms open to receive me, I went to him and received his complete embrace . . . and knew that I had always been a part of him . . . And I knew that I was worthy to be with him, to embrace him. I knew that he was aware of all my sins and faults, but that they didn't matter right now. He just wanted to hold me and share his love with me, and I wanted to share mine with him." (*Embraced*, pgs. 41-42.)

This shockingly untrue confession of Betty's is an abomination to the Lord. God cannot look upon sin with the least degree of allowance! The Lord's prophet Jacob warned us about this when he said: "But behold, hearken ye unto me, and know that by the help of the all-powerful Creator of heaven and earth I can tell you concerning your thoughts, how that ye are beginning to labor in sin, which sin appeareth very abominable unto me, yea, and abominable unto God." (*Jacob 2:5.*) The holy Prophet Alma recorded, "Now they, after being sanctified by the Holy Ghost, having their garments made white, being pure and spotless before God, could not look upon sin save it were with abhorrence . . ." *(Alma 13:12.)* Alma also plainly warned us that: ". . . the Lord cannot look upon sin with the least degree of allowance." *(Alma 45:16.)*

When Betty Eadie says that Jesus was aware of all her sins, but that they "didn't matter right now," is an outright lie. The Lord would never tell anyone that their sins didn't matter. Reading from page 70 of *Embraced by the Light*, Betty says: "If I had broken laws or sinned, I needed to change my heart, and forgive myself . . . In the spirit world they don't see sin as we do here (on earth). All experiences can be positive." *(Embraced,* pgs. 70-71.)

Betty and Curtis Taylor must have the idea that sins and mistakes are one and the same. This is not true. A sin is a violation of God's commandments. Mistakes and errors can be very harmless. For example, the boy Jesus of Nazareth was apprenticed as a carpenter. Undoubtedly Jesus would have mistakenly pounded a nail into the wrong piece of lumber, or maybe cut a board to the wrong length as he was beginning as a carpenter's apprentice. These would have been mistakes and errors which he would have quickly learned from. Jesus Christ however, at no time in His whole eternal life, ever committed a sin! Many people will attempt to minimize sin by referring to sin as a "mistake" or an error. Sins are sins, and a violation of God's law. Mistakes, errors and accidents are unintentional and are not to be construed as sin. To lie about, or to cover up a mistake or an error is a sin, and this happens far more often than it should.

Eadie and Taylor apparently do not fully understand the major differences between sin and error because on page 121 of the "Embraced" book, Betty says that the Lord's angels "cheered when good was done and were saddened by mistakes."

On page 115 and 116, Betty and Curtis try to convince us that a person must sin in order to have the increased ability to counsel and help others. We read, "My perspective of myself was changed, and I saw my sins and shortcomings in a multi-dimensional light . . . Thus the forgiven sin helps me grow and increases my ability to help others." If this were true, then the ones with the most sin, whether repentant or not, would be the greatest counselors and teachers. Ridiculous! A person does not have to experience sin and participate in evil practices in order to be a more qualified counselor. Jesus did not have to sin in order to expound against evil. A Bishop does not have to commit adultery in order to hear the confessions of fornicators and assist them in their complete repentance. Other church leaders, relatives or friends do not need to be liars and thieves in order to aid the sinner back to the "straight and narrow path" of righteousness.

The kingdom of God is governed by celestial laws which are eternal and which can never change. President Joseph Fielding Smith said that: "It should be conceded by all people that since the Almighty governs the entire universe by immutable law, man, who is the greatest of all His creations, must himself be subject to such law. The Lord has stated this truth tersely and convincingly in a revelation to the Church:

'All kingdoms have a law given;

'And there are many kingdoms; for there is no space in the which there is no kingdom; and there is no kingdom in which there is no space, either a greater or a lesser kingdom.

'And unto every kingdom is given a law; and unto every law there are certain bounds also and conditions.

'All beings who abide not in those conditions are not justified." *(D&C 88:36-39.)*

"This truth is self-evident. Thus, it is only reasonable that we should expect the kingdom of God to be governed by law and all who desire to enter there to be subject to law. 'Behold, mine house is a house of order, saith the Lord God, and not a house of confusion.' *(D&C 132:8.)*

"The Lord has given to man a code of laws that we call the gospel of Jesus Christ. Due to lack of inspiration and spiritual guidance, men may differ in relation to these laws and their application, but there can hardly be a dispute in regard to the fact that such laws do exist, and that all who seek entrance into that kingdom are subject to them.

"We teach as fundamentals, first, faith in God the Father, and in the Son, and in the Holy Ghost; second, sincere repentance from all sin; third, baptism by immersion for the remission of sins; fourth, the laying on of hands for the gift of the Holy Ghost. No man may enter into the kingdom of God without first meeting all of these requirements. This is virtually what the Lord declared to Nicodemus when He said: 'Except a man be born of water and of the Spirit, he cannot enter into the kingdom of God." *(John 3:5.)*

"It must be accepted by all who profess belief in our Savior that this edict is true and final. However, in the centuries past and even now in many so-called Christian communities, a wrong application of this doctrine has led to serious errors and unwittingly to the committing of grievous sins. I refer to the doctrine which proclaims that all who in the flesh have not professed belief in our Lord, or heard of Him before death removed them from the earth, are forever damned and without means of escape from the torments of hell. This false conception and application of gospel truth has been a teaching of so-called Christianity from the earliest centuries of our era, but it never was a part of the gospel of Jesus Christ.

"In his *Divine Comedy*, Dante depicts the doctrine of damnation for unfortunate souls who die without a knowledge of Christ, as that doctrine was taught in the thirteenth century. According to the story, Dante is lost in the woods, where he is met by the Roman poet Virgil, who promises to show him the punishment of hell and purgatory, and later he is to have a view of paradise. He follows Virgil through hell and later into Limbo, which is the first circle of hell. Here are confined the souls of those who lived virtuous and honorable lives but who, because they were not baptized, merit punishment and are denied forever the blessings of salvation. As Dante looks upon these miserable souls in the upper stratum of hell and sees, as the story says, 'many and great, both of children, and of women and men,' he marvels.

"His guide asks: 'Thou askest not what spirits are these thou seest?'

"Dante shows a desire to know, so the guide continues: 'I wish thee to know, before thou goest farther, that they sinned not; and though they have merit, it suffices not: for they had not baptism, which is the portal of the faith that thou believest; and seeing they were before Christianity, they worshipped not God aright; and of these am I myself. For such defects, and for no other fault, are we lost; and only in so far afflicted, that without hope we live in desire.' *(Philo M. Buck, Jr., ed., An Anthology of World Literature.* New York: Macmillan Co., 1940. pg. 446.)

"In answer to the earnest inquiry of his mortal guest, who desires to know if any thus punished ever had the privilege of coming forth from this sad condition of torment, the spirit-poet declares that the righteous who had known God from our first parents down to the time of Christ have been exalted. But of these unfortunates who never heard of Christ, he says, 'Be thou assured, no spirit of human kind was ever saved.'

"However, Dante was not the author of this unfortunate and erroneous doctrine. It had come down from the earliest days of apostasy from the true teachings of Jesus Christ.

"The historian Motley, in his *Rise of the Dutch Republic*, relates the following incident as occurring when Christianity was first introduced in Western Europe. Tadbod, a Frisian chieftain, was apparently converted and applied for baptism—and in that day they went down into the water and were immersed. While standing in the water, waiting for the ceremony to be performed, Tadbod turned to the priest, Wolfran, and said: 'Where are my dead forefathers at present?' The unwise priest, with more zeal than wisdom, replied: 'In Hell with all other unbelievers.' 'Mighty well,' replied the heathen chieftain, withdrawing from the water, his ire aroused; 'then will I rather feast with my ancestors in the halls of Woden than dwell with your little starveling band of Christians in Heaven.' *(Vol. 1, pg. 20.)* Under like circumstances, what answer would you have given?

"What a shame it is that this same awful doctrine has come resounding down from that distant day of spiritual darkness and has made to ring its terrible peal of torment repeatedly in the ears of earnest souls who have sought the salvation of loved ones who have gone before. Well do I remember the anguish in the heart of an earnest, loving mother who was told by a well-meaning but misguided priest that her dead infant was eternally lost because the child had not been christened.

"I was visiting at the home of this mother, and she related the following story. Several years before, she had lost a little child. He had not been taken to the minister for sprinkling and had, in that condition, died. The parents sought their minister and asked him to conduct the funeral and give their little one Christian burial; however, this humble request was solemnly, but nonetheless brutally, denied. The parents were told the child was forever lost. Heartbroken, they laid their little child away as an outcast might have been buried, without the rites of that church and without 'Christian burial.' How the hearts of those fond parents ached; how their feelings were torn asunder!

"For several years this mother, with faith in the teachings of that priest, suffered the most acute mental agony. She knew it was not the fault of her infant that he had not been christened. He was innocent of any wrong. Was not that wrong her own? And in her mind, because of this false teaching, was not she responsible for the eternal suffering of that little one? She felt as the repentant murderer who could not restore the life he had taken, and in the anguish of soul she suffered the punishment of the damned.

"It was a happy day when I came to the home of this tormented mother. Even now I can see the joy that came into her tormented face when I explained to her that this doctrine was false—as false as the depths of hell whence it came. I taught her this was not the doctrine of Jesus Christ, who loved little children and declared that they belonged to the kingdom of heaven. I read to her from the *Book of Mormon* the words of Mormon to his son Moroni *(Moroni 8)* and explained that the Lord had revealed to Joseph Smith that 'all children who die before they arrive at the years of accountability'—that is, eight years—'are saved in the celestial kingdom of heaven.' *(Documentary History of the Church, vol. 2, pg. 381.)* Yes, the Lord has made it known in this glorious day of restoration:

'All who have died without a knowledge of this Gospel, who would have received it if they had been permitted to tarry, shall be heirs of the celestial kingdom of God; also all that shall die henceforth without a knowledge of it, who would have received it with all their hearts.' *(DHC, vol. 2, pg. 280.)*

"The gospel of Christ is the gospel of mercy. It is also the gospel of justice. It must be so, for it comes from a God of mercy, not from a cruel monster, as some religionists still believe and erroneously declare that:

'By the decree of God, for the manifestation of His glory some men and angels are predestined unto everlasting life, and others foreordained to everlasting death. These angels and men, thus predestined and foreordained, are particularly and unchangeably designed; and their number is so certain and definite that it cannot be either increased or diminished.'

"Is it not horrible to contemplate that gospel truth has been perverted and defiled until it has become such an abomination? Justice, as well as mercy, pleads for the dead who have died without a knowledge of the gospel. How could justice be administered if all the untold multitudes who have died without knowledge of Jesus Christ should be everlastingly consigned, without hope, to the damnation of hell, even though their torment be in the first circle of the place of the damned?

"The scriptures say, 'Justice and judgment are the habitation of thy throne: mercy and truth shall go before thy face.' *(Ps. 89:14.)*

"The mercy and the love of a just God are reaching out after all His children. In the restoration of the gospel through the Prophet Joseph Smith, the Lord renewed His proclamation of salvation to the dead; He has declared:

'. . . Let your hearts rejoice, and be exceedingly glad. Let the earth break into singing. Let the dead speak forth anthems of eternal praise to the King Immanuel, who hath ordained, before the world was, that which would enable us to redeem them out of their prison; for the prisoners shall go free.'" *(D&C 128:22.) (Joseph Fielding Smith, Passage to Light, 1979, pgs. 133-139.)*

Chapter Eight

Betty Becomes A Rose

A most amazing occurrence is related by Betty to her writer Curtis Taylor, about the rose she observed on her "fantasy tour" through the galaxies. Let's examine this fairy tale in Betty Eadie's own words: "As I approached the water, I noticed a rose near me that seemed to stand out from the other flowers . . . It was gently swaying to faint music and (the rose) was singing praises to the Lord with sweet tones . . . and I wanted to experience its life, to step into it and feel its spirit . . . I seemed to be able to see down into it . . . as though my vision allowed me to penetrate the rose's deepest parts . . . I felt the rose's presence around me, as if I were actually inside and part of the flower. I experienced it as if I <u>were</u> the flower . . . the music in my flower came from its individual parts, that its petals produced their own tones . . . I felt God in the plant, in me, his love pouring into us. We were all one!" (*Embraced,* pgs. 80-81.)

Betty finished this make-believe tale by saying, "I will never forget the rose that I was." This imaginary flower episode sounds like it was taken directly from the "Wizard of Oz" script. Singing flowers which are half-human and half-flower are not a part of the orderly kingdom of God. Our perfectly refined spirit bodies cannot take the form of a flower or any other of God's creations. If everything created by our Father in heaven was formed and created spiritually first, and each creation has a spirit of its own, then to change form and enter that creation would mean that you would be displacing its own unique spirit. It makes no sense, and there would be no purpose to it. For what reason would the Lord have Betty turn into a rose? It is just another "Eadie-ite" fabrication which did not occur. Does Betty actually truly believe in her heart that (as she said in her own word) God and the rose and Betty became as one, inside of a flower? The Lord has a perfected, resurrected and celestially perfect body of flesh and bone. His spirit and His body are one in the eternities. His body and spirit did not join Betty inside of a singing flower. It is foolish to even consider such a ridiculous idea. Betty professes that it is the "gospel truth." She swears it actually happened. It is difficult not to feel a great deal of pity for Betty Eadie and Curtis for concocting a book of falsehoods and heresy; apparently with no remorse for their false publication which has been read by millions of unsuspecting and naive "truth-seekers." People who might have purchased *Embraced by the Light* in order to fulfill a spiritual void in their lives might believe the many false ideas and untruths found in the book.

Let's read some important words from Elder Milton R. Hunter about the hereafter and what really happens after death. Elder Hunter said: "The age-old question of 'Where do we go when we die?' has been asked by old people and young people among all nations from time immemorial. Many disbelievers, cynics, and atheists today maintain that nothing exists for man beyond the grave—that death is the end. The greatest of all teachers, Jesus Christ, the Son of God, proclaimed an entirely different doctrine. He taught that there is a glorious life beyond the grave in the presence of the Eternal Father, and that by compliance with certain laws we may go there and enjoy it. For example, Nicodemus, a ruler of the Jews, came unto Jesus at night and in the course of their conversation, Jesus declared:

'Verily, verily, I say unto thee, except a man be born of water and of the Spirit, he cannot enter into the kingdom of God.' *(John 3:5.)*

"The Savior revealed to Joseph Smith, a modern prophet:

'Take upon you the name of Christ . . .

'And as many as repent and are baptized in my name, which is Jesus Christ, and endure to the end, the same shall be saved.

'Behold, Jesus Christ is the name which is given of the Father, and there is none other name given whereby man can be saved.' *(D&C 18:21-23.)*

"On a certain occasion, a dear friend of the Master in Palestine was very ill. His sisters, Martha and Mary, sent for Jesus to come and heal their brother. The Savior did not come for a few days, and when He did come Lazarus had been dead and buried for four days. Martha was told that Jesus was approaching, and so she hurried out to meet him. She said: 'Lord, if thou hadst been here, my brother had not died . . .

'Jesus said unto her, Thy brother shall arise again.

'Martha saith unto him, I know he shall rise again in the resurrection of the last day.

"Jesus replied: 'I am the resurrection, and the life; he that believeth in me, though he were dead, yet shall he live:

'And whosoever liveth and believeth in me shall never die. Believest thou this?' *(John 11:21-26.)*

"The night before His crucifixion, Jesus gave His apostles additional information regarding His Father's kingdom. He said to them:

'In my Father's house are many mansions: if it were not so, I would have told you. I go now to prepare a place for you.

'And if I go and prepare a place for you, I will come again, and receive you unto Myself; that where I am, there ye may be also.' *(John 14:2-3.)*

"What is death? It is nothing more than the separation of the spiritual body from the physical body. The physical tabernacle becomes diseased, worn, and aged, and therefore, no longer a fit home for the spirit. Thus the spirit—the real person, in which all the good deeds committed, also the bad deeds committed, the personality—goes on alive as a spirit personage in the spirit world. Some departed spirits go to paradise, a place of peace and happiness and progress. Others go to a spirit prison. Certain prophets have termed it a hell. The Apostle Peter proclaimed that Christ who suffered death for our sins "went and preached unto the spirits in prison" *(1 Pet. 3:19)*, who had been there from the time they were drowned in the flood in Noah's day.

"Thus they were in the spirit prison for nearly twenty-five hundred years, because they had rejected the gospel of Jesus Christ and had lived wicked lives.

"John the Revelator saw in vision the resurrection and judgement of the human family. He described it as follows:

'And I saw the dead, small and great stand before God; and the books were opened, which is the book of life: and the dead were judged out of those things which were written in the books, according to their works.

'And the sea gave up the dead which were in it; and death and hell delivered up the dead which were in them; and they were judged every man according to their works.' *(Rev. 20:12-13.)*

"The ancient American prophets taught that there would be a universal resurrection. Amulek stated: '. . . the day cometh that all shall rise from the dead and stand before God, and be judged according to their works.' *(Al. 11:41.)*

"Jacob, the brother of Nephi, described the judgement day: 'Wherefore, we shall have a perfect knowledge of all our guilt, and our uncleanness and our nakedness; and the righteous shall have a perfect knowledge of their enjoyment, and their righteousness, being clothed with purity, yea, even with the robe of righteousness.' *(2 Ne. 9:14.)*

"The most profound and marvelous revelations that exist on life after death and the final destiny of man were received by the Prophet Joseph Smith. They are recorded in Sections 76, 88, 131, and 132 of the Doctrine and Covenants. In addition, other visions he had on the immortality of man are also recorded in the Doctrine and Covenants.

"God revealed to the Prophet that there are three degrees of glory—the celestial, the terrestrial, and the telestial. If a person's body at the resurrection is quickened by a portion of the celestial glory,' he shall later receive a fullness of that glory. The same holds true for the other two degrees of glory. On February 16, 1832, Joseph Smith and Sidney Rigdon were translating the Bible at Hiram, Ohio, when they had a marvelous vision.

'And while we meditated upon these things, the Lord touched the eyes of our understandings and they were opened, and the glory of the Lord shone around about.

'And we beheld the glory of the Son, on the right hand of the Father, and received of His fullness;

'And saw the holy angels, and them who are sanctified before His throne, worshipping God, and the Lamb, who worship Him forever and ever.

'And now, after the many testimonies which have been given of Him, this is the testimony, last of all, which we give of Him: That He lives!

'For we saw Him, even on the right hand of God; and we heard the voice bearing record that He is the Only Begotten of the Father—

'That by Him, and through Him . . . the worlds are and were created, and the inhabitants thereof are begotten sons and daughters unto God.' *(D&C 76:19-24.)*

"Who will go to the celestial degree of glory and live with the Father and the Son?

"From another vision of celestial glory had by Joseph Smith, we receive the following information:

'And I also beheld that all children who die before they arrive at the years of accountability, are saved in the celestial kingdom of heaven.' *(Documentary History of the Church, Vol. 2, pg. 381.)*

"By revelation the Lord declared age eight as the age of accountability for little children. *(D&C 68:27.)*

"In addition to little children, others who go to the celestial glory are those who receive a testimony of Jesus, in other words, the gospel of Jesus Christ. They must be baptized by immersion in water and receive the holy Ghost by one having authority. Also, they must keep the commandments, and be those who are 'overcome by faith and are sealed by the Holy

Spirit of promise, which the Father sheds forth upon all those who are just and true.' *(D&C 76:53.)*

"Certainly many of the people in celestial glory will be holders of the holy Melchizedek Priesthood.

'In the celestial glory there are three heavens or degrees;

'And in order to obtain the highest, a man must enter into this order of the priesthood (meaning the new and everlasting covenant of marriage);

'If he does not, he cannot obtain it.

'He may enter into the other, but that is the end of his kingdom; he cannot have an increase.' *(D&C 131:1-14.)*

"The Lord has declared that the honorable people of the earth who do not accept the true gospel of Jesus Christ will go to the terrestrial glory.

"The wicked people of the earth who have not denied the Holy Ghost—'They who are thrust down to hell until the last resurrection'—will be assigned to the telestial glory.

"The people who commit the unpardonable sins of denying the Holy Ghost or shedding innocent blood shall be cast off with the devil and die the second death.

"Where do we go when we die? It depends on how we live while here in mortality, and how much light and truth we receive, and how much opportunity we have had. Also, for those who have not had a chance to hear the gospel while here in mortality, they will have an opportunity in the spirit world and temple work will be done for them. The Lord revealed to the Prophet Joseph Smith:

'All who have died without a knowledge of this Gospel, who would have received it if they had been permitted to tarry, shall be heirs to the celestial kingdom of God: Also all that shall die henceforth without a knowledge of it, who would have received it with all their hearts, shall be heirs of the kingdom for I, the Lord, will judge all men . . . according to the desires of their hearts.'" *(DHC, vol. 2, pg. 380.)*

Betty's idea about having her spirit soul enter into a rose must have been extracted from a book written in the early 1900s titled *Anne of Avonlea (Anne of Green Gables)* by the author, L.M. Montgomery. On page 323, Lucy Maud Montgomery writes: "I read somewhere once that souls were like flowers," said Priscilla. "Then your soul is a golden narcissus," said Anne, "and Diana's is like a red, red rose. Jane's is an apple blossom, pink and wholesome and sweet." "And your own is a white violet, with purple streaks in its heart," finished Priscilla. (Montgomery, L. M., 1874-1942. Crown Publishers, Inc., New York, NY.)

The "Anne of Avonlea" and *Anne of Green Gables* stories are very popular and have been read by many millions of young women for many years. Wherever Betty Eadie, Curtis Taylor and the other "Eadie-ite" ghost writers borrowed their ideas from is really of no concern. What is of great importance for all to realize is that it certainly did not occur as Betty testifies. Betty's spirit did not enter a "singing rose" in the hereafter. Nor did Jesus enter that rose with Betty as she boastfully claims. It's a preposterous lie . . . and the authors know it!

Chapter Nine

Unprepared For The Spirit World

Many millions of those who die enter the afterlife, or the spirit world extremely unprepared. Many enter death in an unrepentant stage of their eternal life and are not ready to continue their eternal progression.

"Looms in the Library" is a chapter heading which begins on page 72 of *Embraced by the Light* where Betty Eadie and Curtis write: ". . . I developed a relationship and knowledge of the Savior . . . He knew what I was capable of understanding and he carefully prepared me to absorb all the knowledge . . . In the spirit world no one is made to feel uncomfortable by being forced to do or accept things for which they are not prepared." How wrong you are Betty!

Spirit personages who have been separated from the physical bodies through death enter the spirit world which the Savior spoke about to the thief on the cross. A person who was employed on earth, no longer has the job. The person who abused his body with alcohol, tobacco and other addictive and damaging drugs no longer is able to have access to these poisons . . . even though their spirit mind and soul is still addicted and craves the drugs. Intimacy and sexual desires of the physical body may still exist but could be forbidden in the spirit world.

Again, Betty said that, "In the spirit world no one is made to feel uncomfortable by being forced to do or accept things for which they are not prepared." As you can easily understand, there are masses of people who go to their deaths unprepared and in an untimely fashion . . . who will be forced to behave and act very much differently than they were ever accustomed to doing here upon the earth. Of course, Betty did not visit the spirit world in November of 1973, and even if she would have, she wouldn't return with such faulty information which she claims came directly from the Lord.

Now the only explanation for all the many pages of misinformation would be Betty Eadie's next statement on the same page 72, in her next paragraph when she said, "I'll never forget the Lord's sense of humor, which was as delightful and quick as any here—far more so. Nobody could out-do his humor." On the next page Betty has the gall to make the following demeaning assertions about our Lord. She says, "I knew him . . . there was also an element of authority. He was tender and good natured, but also responsible . . . he would never misuse his authority . . . (and) never even desire to do so." Did Betty Eadie actually question that Jesus would misuse His authority? In Betty's opinion, did He have just a minor element of authority? Did Betty wonder if Christ was responsible? This is blasphemy in one of its highest forms. A mockery of God, and a demeaning "put-down" of the Savior of the world . . . as if Betty's scrutiny and verification was important to the Lord. Does God really need Betty Eadie's personal stamp of approval? Did she really believe that Jesus Christ had "a desire to misuse His authority?" This is most amazing . . . and very dangerous for Betty to presuppose such beliefs and even to entertain such thoughts about our Savior!

A great disciple of Christ, Sterling W. Sill, spoke of the importance of preparing for entrance into the spirit world. We read that:

"Two of the most important events in life are birth and death. And what a thrilling thing it is to be well born, to have goodly parents and live in a godly home! But it may be even more important to die well.

"Sometimes we miss one of our best opportunities—to learn to die well—because we think of death as unpleasant. And because we don't like to think about unpleasant things, we sometimes close our minds and turn away our faces. But death doesn't cease to exist just because it is ignored. The ancient Egyptians had a much more logical way of handling this situation when on their great festive occasions they kept constantly on display before the revelers the skeleton of a dead man. That is, they held up this great image of death before themselves that each one might be continually and constantly reminded that some day he would die.

"Now I don't want to frighten anyone unduly, but I would like to point out as gently and as kindly as I can that someday this tremendously important experience of our mortal estate will come to its end. Someone has said that judging by the past there will be very few of us who get out of this world alive. From the very beginning of life, each one of us lives under an irrevocable, unchangeable death sentence, with a guarantee that it will be carried out. The Lord has given us this maximum notice to enable us to adequately prepare for it. And one man indicated this certainly by an inscription on his tombstone which said, 'I knew it would happen!'

"The other night I reread the old Grecian tragedy written around the fall of Athens. A Roman general had captured an Athenian philosopher and had told him that he meant to put him to death. The Athenian didn't seem very disturbed and so the Roman thought that probably he didn't understand. And so he said to the Athenian that maybe he didn't know what it meant to die. The Athenian said that he thought he understood it better than the Roman did. And then he said to the Roman, 'Thou dost not know what it means to die, for thou dost not know what it means to live. To die is to begin to live. It is to end all stale and weary work to begin a nobler and a better life. It is to leave deceitful knaves for the society of gods and goodness!

"And it has been said that the most important event in life is death. We live to die and then we die to live. Death is a kind of graduation day for life. It is our only means of entrance to our eternal lives. And it seems to me to be a very helpful procedure to spend a little time preliving our death. That is, what kind of person would you like to be when the last hour of your life arrives?

"The last hour is the key hour. That is the hour that judges all of the other hours. No one can tell whether or not his life has been successful until his last hour. As Sophocles said, 'We must wait till evening to know how pleasant the day has been.'

"Certainly no one could write the life story of Jesus of Nazareth or Judas Iscariot without knowing what happened during their last hour. And I would like to tell you about some of the things that one man thought about during his last hour. This is the old legendary story of Faust. Dr. John Faust died in Wittenberg, Germany in the year 1540. But twenty-four years before his death, he sold his soul to Satan. He said to Satan, 'If you will aid me for twenty-four years, punishing my enemies and helping my friends, at the end of that time, I will forever deliver up my soul.'

"Now at that time that seemed like a good idea to Faust. Twenty-four years was a long time. Twenty-four years may last forever. And anyway, what difference did it make what happened after twenty-four years? But Satan, with better perspective said, "I will wait on Faustus while he lives and he shall buy my service with his soul."

"And then the twenty-four years began, and Faust had every experience of good and bad. But almost before he was aware, it was said to Faust as it must be said to everyone of us, 'Thine hour is come.' Now this is the first time that he had ever thought about the consequences of what he was doing. Only now did he discover how badly he had cheated himself. Then he wanted to revoke the bargain, but that was impossible. And then he prayed and he said, 'Oh God, if thou canst have no mercy on my soul, at least grant some end of my incessant pain. Let Faustus live in hell a thousand years or even a hundred thousand, but at last be saved!'

"But he knew that, according to his own bargain, even this could never be. And then during his last hour he sat and watched the clock tick off the seconds and finally, just as the hour struck, the last words of Faust before he died were: 'Faustus is gone to hell!'

"Now if Faust had lived his last hour first, he never would have permitted himself to come to this unprofitable place. I have a relative who, when she reads a novel, always reads the last chapter first. She wants to know before she begins where she is going to be when she gets through. And that is a pretty good idea for life.

"Now I don't know what it would be like if we sometime discovered that we had missed the goal of life and had allowed ourselves to become only telestial souls. I do know that it would be as far below the celestial as the twinkle of a tiny star is below the blaze of the noonday sun. We know quite a lot about the celestial kingdom. We know that it is the place which God has prepared for those who are valiant in His service and keep all of His commandments. We know quite a lot about celestial beings, as we have had a number of them appear to us upon this earth. And each time they have come, those who have received them have said they are impossible to describe.

"When the Prophet Joseph Smith had his vision of the Father and the Son, he said, 'Their brightness and glory defy all description.' *(Joseph Smith 2:17.)* That is, we don't have any background of knowledge; there isn't a vocabulary to use in describing a celestial accomplishment.

"There are some things that we can't describe even in this life. For example, if I tried to describe to you the look in my little granddaughter's eyes on Christmas morning, when she's radiant and expectant and something is shining out through her face, I might have difficulty telling you about it even though I can understand it. I might try by saying she has a light in her eye, or her face beams, or her countenance is aglow. Now none of those things are true, actually. Her eyes are the same color, the same shape, the same size as they were before. But something is shining out through her face that is indescribable.

"The Prophet Joseph Smith tried to describe the resurrected Jesus as he saw Him in the Kirtland Temple on April 3, 1836. And he said, 'His eyes were as a flame of fire.' *(D&C 110:3.)* It isn't a twinkle anymore; I suppose it is now magnified a few million times. I suppose that actually there wasn't any fire there at all, any more than there is a light in my granddaughter's eyes. He is trying to describe something which can't be described. He said, 'His face shown above the brightness of the sun;' and that is pretty bright.

"We sometimes imagine that Jesus is different than we are, but the Prophet Joseph Smith tried to describe his some fifteen or sixteen visits with the angel Moroni. Moroni was a soldier who lived upon our continent. For the last thirty-seven years of his life he lived alone. He said, 'My father hath been slain as well as all my kinfolks, I have not friends nor whither to go.' 'Wherefore,' said he, 'I wander whithersoever I can for the safety of mine own life.' *(Morm. 8:5, Moro. 1:3.)*

"He didn't have a warm bathroom to go into every morning or someone to get him a good breakfast or provide him with clean clothing. We might imagine that during these many long and lonely years he had allowed his personality to run down a little bit. And then we see him for the last time as he stood there on the edge of his grave, writing us his last paragraph. In closing his great book he said, 'And now I bid unto all, farewell. I soon go to rest in the paradise of God, until my spirit and body shall again reunite, and I am brought forth triumphant through the air, to meet you before the pleasing bar of the great Jehovah, the Eternal Judge of both quick and dead.' *(Moro. 10:34.)*

"And then there followed a long silence of fourteen centuries. For 1,403 years we heard nothing more, until on the night of September 21, 1823, this same old man, now resurrected and glorified, stood by the bedside of Joseph Smith. And the Prophet tried to describe him as he then appeared. And while he said that it was impossible, yet he tried. And here are some of the phrases he used. He said, 'His whole person was glorious beyond description, and his countenance truly like lightning.' *(Joseph Smith 2:21.)*

"We all know the things that we do to make this body a pleasant habitation. We bathe it and keep it clean, we dress it in the most appropriate clothing. Sometimes we ornament it with jewelry. If we're very wealthy we buy necklaces and bracelets and diamond rings and other things to make this body sparkle and shine and make it a pleasant place. Sometimes we work on it a little bit with cosmetics and eyebrow tweezers, but we keep working at it all the time.

"Now if you think it would be pleasant to be dressed in expensive clothing, what do you think it would be like sometime to be dressed in an expensive body—that shines like the sun, one that is beautiful beyond all comprehension, with quickened senses, amplified powers of perception, and vastly increased capacity for love, understanding, and happiness. And we might just keep in mind that God runs the most effective beauty parlor ever known in the world.

"Socrates was a very homely man, and he prayed to the Lord and said, 'Make me beautiful within.' We have all seen plain people who have been made beautiful by the working of a radiant spirituality. A godly spirit will make the plainest body beautiful. Great mental and spiritual qualities transform our bodies into their likeness.

"And so we come back to the place where we began. What a thrilling experience that we may live well, enabling us to die well and then live with God in the celestial kingdom throughout eternity. The apostle Paul said, we die, 'and, behold, we live.'" (2 Cor. 6:9.)

(Sterling W. Sill, *Passage to Light,* 1979, pgs. 52-57.)

Chapter Ten

Betty's Three Monks

I n order to appeal to the many people who profess membership in the Catholic church, Betty and Curtis invented three monks. Beginning on page 30 of *Embraced by the Light,* Betty said that three monks "suddenly appeared at my side. They wore beautiful, light brown robes, and one of them had a hood on the back of his head. Each wore a gold-braided belt that was tied about the waist with the ends hanging down . . . The men appeared to be about seventy or eighty years old, but . . . the impression came to me that they were much older . . . that they were ancient." *(Embraced, 30-31.)*

Betty said that they spoke to her and told her that they had been with her for eternities. She said, "Then I began to see images in my mind . . . of my relationship with these men . . . and I became excited . . . As this feeling came over me, I sensed their deep love and concern." Betty claims that her three monks communicated with her by "telepathy," with their minds, and that she "felt their emotions and intent(s) . . . and felt their love . . . and experienced their feelings. Betty said, ". . . this filled me with joy because they loved me so much." *(Embraced, 31-32.)*

There is no scriptural reference to "monks" anywhere to be found. The word "monk" was translated from the Greek word "monos" which means to "be alone." The Webster's Dictionary defines a "monk" as a man who retires to live in solitary self-denial for religious reasons. A man who joins a religious order living in retirement according to a rule and under vows of poverty, obedience, and chastity.

It is not exactly clear who Eadie and Taylor were attempting to depict with their "three monks" sighting. It could have been a subtle reference to the appearance of the ancient prophets of the Lord; Peter, James and John when they appeared to the Prophet Joseph Smith on the banks of the Susquehanna River and conferred the Holy Melchizedek Priesthood upon Joseph Smith and Oliver Cowdery in June of 1829. *(D&C 27:12, D&C 128:20, JS-H 1:72.)* Maybe Betty and Curtis were alluding to their "three monks" as a special appearance of the Three Nephites; or maybe to the Father, the Son and the Holy Ghost!

In any event, there were not "three monks" as they claim. Our Father in heaven does not use "monks" to perform His bidding. There is no such priesthood office or calling as "monk" in God's earthly church or in the heavenly realms.

There are, however, angels which may be assigned to us by our loving and protective Father in heaven. The necessity for guardian angels was published in the Relief Society Magazine. It read that when Satan was banished from heaven, he made his way to earth with his hosts of banished spirits. He evidently knew that none of the valiant spirits from heaven would have any inclination for any earthly existence if the privilege of being "added upon" or receiving bodies could not be obtained. Two of Lucifer's greatest objectives were the prevention of mortal life and the destruction of that life. To accomplish the first, he attempted to have Adam and Eve perpetually separated, and to accomplish the second, he has sought by disease, individual strife, abortion and the destruction of war to depopulate the earth.

Satan has no respect for God's authority but he stands in fearful and submissive awe of the power that Divinity has for the enforcement of authority. The evil one has reason to know what it means to come in conflict with the angels.

The prince of darkness is held in check by the knowledge that the same authority and power which cast one of his spirits out of man and permitted the evil spirits to possess the bodies of swine could banish him and all his hosts from the face of the earth. If angels were needed as a power to preserve heaven from the grasps of Satan, how could the children of our Father be expected to survive on earth among the condemned without the protective presence of messengers from on high?

Group Guardianship. The government of God provides for the meeting of emergencies by having in readiness or subject to call, valiant spirits for the defense of heaven's cause—beings trained in obedience through the law of love and loyalty; beings in whose presence wickedness quails and the emissaries of unrighteousness grow weak. These defenders of righteousness may not be visible, though they be present on earth in multitudes and are part of heaven's power.

Individual Guardianship. Among the duties of guardian angels are private revelation, protection, comfort, admonition, and watchfulness of the intentions and actions of enemies. The Angel Moroni, the guardian of the plates from which the *Book of Mormon* was translated, revealed the existence and place of deposit to the Prophet Joseph Smith. The Angel Gabriel revealed to Elisabeth's husband her foreordained motherhood, and this same angel announced to Mary her marvelous mission. Some angel with special interest in the virgin mother's welfare and undoubtedly by appointment, saved Mary from being misunderstood by her espoused husband, who stood between her and the contumely of society in obedience to Divine instruction. The guardian angel of Jesus was on the alert at the councils of the murderous Herod, read his thoughts, and reported his intentions to the foster father of the Babe of Bethlehem.

Satan used his scriptural knowledge of the doctrine of guardian angels in an attempt to ensnare the Savior. After the temptation was over, angels "ministered to Him." As to whether these angels witnessed the "temptation" contest, as did the friends and Father of the Redeemer witness the crime of crimes at Calvary, we do not know, but this we know, that these angels brought the comfort needed by one who had fasted, fought and won.

The Value of the Guardian Angel Idea. A prominent physician, in discussing religion made this remark, "I am glad my parents taught me the doctrine of guardian angels; it steadied my early life over many a chasm of temptation. The very idea itself is a protection to youth.

"I need no argument to prove to me that to live in thought only with pure, powerful protectors will make of one something more than it is possible to be without the thought. But guardian angels are something more than imaginations growing out of beliefs. They are real, tangible entities whose influence may be felt and whose words may be exercised within the field of their appointment."

The nursery rhyme, "Lie still, my babe, and sweetly slumber, Holy angels guard thy bed," is more than poetry, it is truth—God's truth. And if the mother's eyes were opened as were the eyes of the servant of Elisha, she would see by vision what she now sees by faith. *(The Relief Society Magazine, Vol 10,* pgs 41-43.)

Chapter Eleven

Did Betty Fly to Other Worlds?

A continuation of Betty Eadie's hoax resumes on page 86 of *Embraced by the Light*. The chapter is entitled "Many Worlds." It should be made clear to all readers that Betty originally learned of other worlds which our Father in heaven created through her earlier conversion and baptism into The Church of Jesus Christ of Latter-day Saints (commonly referred to as the Mormon Church).

Betty and Curtis are very familiar with the scriptures referring to "other worlds" such as Moses 1:33, 35 which reads, "And worlds without number have I created; and I also created them for mine own purpose; and by the Son I created them, which is mine Only Begotten . . . For behold, there are many worlds that have passed away by the word of My power. And there are many that now stand, and innumerable are they unto man; but all things are numbered unto Me, for they are mine and I know them."

God has created far too many worlds for man to even imagine; and all through His beloved Son, Jesus Christ, as was revealed to the great Prophet Moses. Betty Eadie and Curtis Taylor claim that this information was revealed to her in the

"Embraced" book which they published in the year 1992. Read how Betty, just a few years ago, said that this knowledge came to her. Eadie says, "My memory was opened further than before, reaching back beyond the creation of our earth into eternities past. I remembered that God was the creator of many worlds, galaxies and realms beyond our understanding, and I wanted to see them. As the desire came, my thoughts gave me power, and I drifted away from the garden, escorted this time by two different beings of light who then became my guides. Our spiritual bodies floated away from friends and into the blackness of space." *(Embraced,* 86.)

It is helpful to understand that Betty Eadie and Curtis Taylor had many other "Eadie-ites" assist, write, draft, edit, imagine and invent much of *Embraced by the Light.* This is why there is so much of the Mormon influence in the book's structure. Betty and Curtis and Nancy and Jane and Marilyn and Joe and Mikel and Brian and many others collaborated as a group to rework the fictional experience Betty Eadie pretends to have gone through two decades ago. Some of the "Eadie-ite" helpers purposely chose not to attach their personal names to the book, *Embraced by the Light,* because they knew in their hearts it wasn't right or true.

The amazing space travel story gets even more farfetched. Referring again to page 86 through 88, Betty is quoted as saying: "Our speed increased, and I felt the exhilaration of flight. I could do whatever I wanted, go wherever I desired, go fast—incredibly fast—or go slow . . . I seemed to be gone for weeks, even months, visiting the many creations of God . . . I traveled to many other worlds—earths like our own but more glorious, and always filled with loving, intelligent people . . . I traveled tremendous distances, knowing that the stars I saw were not visible from earth. I saw galaxies and traveled to them with ease and almost instantaneous speed, visiting their worlds and meeting more children of our God . . . I knew that

I had been to these places before . . . God didn't have to show me these other worlds. In his mercy, I saw worlds that our most powerful telescopes could never see." *(Embraced,* pgs. 86-88.)

In some parts of the book, Betty says she was only near-death. In other parts of the "Embraced" book, Betty claims to have been absolutely dead for a total of four hours; and then in the "Many Worlds" chapter, she said she "seemed to have been gone for weeks, even months." The contradictions are almost beyond belief. Heavenly Father told Moses that He had created numberless concourses of worlds and heavens, but He only showed Moses this earth, its land and inhabitants. However, if we are to believe Betty Eadie and the "Eadie-ites" we must believe that Our Father showed Betty never before seen creations, worlds and human inhabitants and permitted her to visit worlds and their peoples. Why was Betty able to experience so much more than Moses? This is just too great of a hoax. It did not happen and Betty knows it; in her heart of hearts, she knows it. Only through a hypnotic trance could a person actually believe that this happened to her, and Betty admits to being a hypnotist with a knowledge of self-hypnosis.

A really astounding portion of this inter-galactic tour Betty relates to us is on page 87 of *Embraced by the Light* where she must have taken a scene from Steven Spielberg's blockbuster movie, "Close Encounters of the Third Kind" at the very end when the aliens connected with earthlings in the film. Betty says, "I heard a soft, pleasant sound, a distant but comforting sound that made me happy. It was a tone, similar to a tone of music, but was universal and seemed to fill all the space around me. It was followed by another tone at a different pitch, and soon I noticed something of a melody—a vast, cosmic song that soothed and comforted me. The tones produced soft vibrations, and as they touched me I knew that they possessed the power to heal."

This is straight from the big screen, and by another producer and director. His name is Steven Spielberg and he released this new-age, space-age tone idea many years before you did. Admit it; don't take credit for it. Far too many people saw "Close Encounters" for Betty to try and make us believe that this is a new revelation from God to her.

Chapter Twelve

Good Intentions Gone Bad

I t appears certain that many of the misconceptions Betty Eadie and Curtis Taylor have put forth as true experiences are nothing more than a feeble, but false attempt to do good. However, a falsehood is a lie no matter how good a person's intentions may be. What one person feels is good for another might be very damaging and seriously detrimental to all.

Two very serious fallacies that Betty and Curtis display as truth and as actual experiences are found on pages 94-96 of *Embraced by the Light*. Read the words, and listen to the utterly outrageous premise of which Betty boasts: ". . . my attention turned to the other spirits making preparations to go to earth. One exceptionally brilliant and dynamic spirit was just entering his mother's womb. He had chosen to enter this world mentally handicapped."

Can you believe this?! Keep reading, it gets worse! "He (the mentally retarded baby) was very excited about this opportunity and was aware of the growth he and his parents would achieve. The three of them had . . . planned for this arrangement long before." This is incredible, Betty. No one would choose to live their whole life with a physical, mental or spiritual handicap . . . especially if it were only to "help another person grow and develop" as you claim. Our righteous and Eternal Father in heaven knows who will live with deformities; either from accidents, disease or genetics, but pre-mortal spirits do not choose these circumstances; nor do they choose the manner or time of their deaths.

Is Betty's belief that if she tells someone that lives with a handicap that they chose it themselves before they were born, they will more readily accept it and be happier with their lot in life? Should the handicapped then not attempt to try and better themselves, even to reach to overcome a particular handicap because it was predestined to be permanent? This obviates God's plan of salvation for each of us in mortality. Does Betty believe that each pre-mortal soul chose their own height, weight, and hair color? How about race and the color of each person's skin at birth . . . did we choose that? As if in a cafeteria line, did we each choose poverty over wealth, disease over health? Of course not. To preach this phony philosophy as "direct knowledge" from Christ is nothing less than heresy!

Mrs. Eadie proceeds to falsely instruct us that Jesus revealed to her that, ". . . spirits can choose to enter their mother's body at any stage of her pregnancy." *(Embraced, pg. 95.)* If this were true, and pre-mortal spirit souls were able to choose when they entered the womb, then many abortions which occurred prior to the spirit entry would not really be a wrongful death. For example, if a mother chose to abort her fetus in the second trimester of her pregnancy, but the baby spirit had not chosen to enter her womb until the seventh month, then no evil crime against God would have been committed. Why would any intelligent, pre-mortal baby spirit ever choose to enter the womb until the moment of birth . . . if there was the slightest possibility that the mother could abort. This makes no sense, Betty, and our Father in heaven would not permit it. When two human spirits act in the manner to procreate another human spirit, whether intentionally or not, they join with God and creation begins at that time. Not three months later, or six months, or nine months later . . . but at the time when the couple actively procreates a newly formed human, they procreate with God the spirit arrival of a new soul at that same instant.

Betty Eadie and her mentor, Curtis Taylor, and others also permitted the idea that infant deaths occur for the sole purpose of helping others grow. This is what they said on pages 95 and 96 of their book: "I saw many spirits who would come to the earth only for a short time, living only hours or days after their birth . . . knowing that they had a purpose to fulfill . . . that their deaths had been appointed before their births—as were all of ours . . . and their deaths would provide challenges that would help their parents grow. The grief that comes here is intense but short." No, Betty, the grief is intense and long. Some parents, relatives and friends grow through their unwanted grief . . . but many do not. Some permit their lives and relationships to be damaged and ruined because they do not understand the fullness of the truth about life after death as found in the gospel of Jesus Christ.

Let a really inspired and knowledgeable disciple of our Lord, Bruce R. McConkie, explain about the salvation of little children. Elder McConkie writes, "Among all the glorious gospel verities given of God to His people there is scarcely a doctrine so sweet, so soul satisfying and so soul sanctifying, as the one which proclaims —

"Little children shall be saved. They are alive in Christ and shall have eternal life. For them the family unit will continue, and the fullness of exaltation is theirs. No blessing shall be withheld. They shall rise in immortal glory, grow to full maturity, and live forever in the highest heaven of the celestial kingdom—all through the merits and mercy and grace of the Holy Messiah, all because of the atoning sacrifice of Him who died that we might live.

One of the greatest benefits of the recent addition to the Pearl of Great Price of Joseph Smith's vision of the Celestial Kingdom is the opportunity it affords to study anew the doctrine relative to the salvation of children. There are many valid questions which confront us in this field which are deserving of sound scriptural answers.

"Two scenes showing the infinite love, tenderness, and compassion of the Lord Jesus set the stage for our consideration of the various matters involved in the salvation of children.

"The first scene is set on 'the coast of Judea beyond Jordan.' Great multitudes are before Him; the Pharisees are querulous, seeking to entrap; He has just preached about marriage and the family unit. 'Then there were brought unto Him little children,' Matthew records, 'that He should put His hands on them and pray. And the disciples rebuked them, saying, There is no need, for Jesus hath said, Such shall be saved.

"'But Jesus said, Suffer little children to come unto Me, and forbid them not, for of such is the kingdom of heaven.

"'And He laid hands on them, and departed hence.'" *(Matt. 19:13-15, Inspired Version.)*

"The second scene is portrayed on the American continent. That same Jesus, the Compassionate One, risen and glorified, is ministering among His Nephi kinsmen. He has just prayed as none other had ever done before. 'No tongue can speak, neither can there be written by any man, neither can the hearts of men conceive so great and marvelous things as we both saw and heard Jesus speak,' the Nephi historian records. *(3 Nephi 17:17.)*

"'Then Jesus wept, and said: "Behold your little ones . . .

"'And they saw the heavens open, and they saw angels descending out of heaven as it were in the midst of fire; and they came down and encircled those little ones about, and they were encircled about with fire; and the angels did minister unto them.'" *(3 Nephi 17:23-24.)*

"Now let us record brief answers to the more commonly asked questions about the salvation of children.

What is a child and who are children?

"A child is an adult spirit in a newly born body, a body capable of growing and maturing according to the providences of Him whose spirit children we are. Children are the sons and daughters of God. They lived and dwelt with Him for ages and eons before their mortal birth. They are adults before birth; they are adults at death. Christ himself, the Firstborn of the Father, rose to a state of glory and exaltation before He was ever held by His mother Mary.

What is mortal birth?

"It is the process by which mature, sentient, intelligent beings pass from preexistence into a mortal sphere. It is the process by which we bring from premortality to mortality the traits and talents acquired and developed in our long years of spirit existence. It is the process by which a mortal body is created from the dust of the earth to house an eternal spirit offspring of the Father of us all.

Why are we born upon this earth?

"We come here to gain bodies, bodies of flesh and blood, bodies which—following natural death—we will receive back again in immortality. Those of us who arrive at the years of accountability are here to develop and to be tried and tested, to see if we can so live as to regain the state of innocence and purity which we enjoyed as children, and thereby be qualified to go where God and Christ are.

What is original sin?

"This is the false doctrine that the sin of Adam passes upon all men, and that, therefore, all men—infants included—must be baptized to be saved. It is, however, a fundamental principle of true religion 'that all men will be punished for their own sins, and not for Adam's transgression.' (Second Article of Faith.)

Are children tainted with original sin?

"Absolutely not. There is no such thing as original sin as such is defined in the creeds of Christendom. Such a concept denies the efficacy of the atonement. Our revelation says, 'Every spirit of man was innocent in the beginning'—meaning that spirits started out in a state of purity and innocence in the preexistence—and God having redeemed man from the fall, men became again, in their infant state, innocent before God' (D&C 93:38)—meaning that all children start out their mortal probation in purity and innocence because of the atonement. Our revelations also say, 'The Son of God hath atoned for original guilt, wherein the sins of the parents cannot be answered upon the heads of the children, for they are whole from the foundation of the world.' (Moses 6:54.)

Are children conceived in sin?

"Since there is no such thing as original sin, as that expression is used in modern Christendom, it follows that children are not conceived in sin. They do not come into the world with any taint of impurity whatsoever. When our scriptures say, 'children are conceived in sin,' they are using words in an entirely different way than when the same language is recited in the creeds of the world. The scriptural meaning is that, 'when they begin to grow up, sin conceiveth in their hearts, and they taste the bitter, that they may know to prove the good.' *(Moses 6:55.)*

What about infant baptism?

"Few false doctrines have ever deserved and received such a vigorous and forceful denunciation as that heaped upon infant baptism by the prophet Mormon. When that inspired author inquired of the Lord concerning the baptism of little children, he said, 'Listen to the words of Christ, your Redeemer, your Lord and your God. Behold, I came into the world not to call the righteous but sinners to repentance; the whole need no physician, but they that are sick, wherefore, little children are whole, for they are not capable of committing sin; wherefore the curse of Adam is taken from them in Me, that it hath no power over them.'

"Thereupon, Mormon speaking by the power of the Holy Ghost, taught that 'it is solemn mockery' to baptize little children; that they 'are alive in Christ from the foundation of the world;' that it is awful wickedness to deny the pure mercies of Christ to them; that such a belief sets at naught the power of Christ's redemption; that those who believe such a false concept are 'in the bonds of iniquity' and if cut off while in the thought shall be thrust down to hell; and those who humble themselves and repent and are baptized shall 'be saved with their little children.' *(Moroni 8:8-25.)*

Are all little children saved automatically in the celestial kingdom?

"To this question the answer is a thunderous **yes**, which echoes and re-echoes from one end of heaven to the other.

Jesus taught it to His disciples. Mormon said it over and over again. Many of the prophets have spoken about it, and it is implicit in the whole plan of salvation. If it were not so, the redemption would not be infinite in its application. And so, as we would expect, Joseph Smith's vision of the Celestial Kingdom contains this statement: 'And I also beheld that all children who die before they reach the years of accountability are saved in the celestial kingdom of heaven.'

"It is sometimes asked if this applies to children of all races, and of course the answer is that when the revelation says all children, it means all children. There is no restriction as to race, kindred, tongue. Little children are little children and they are all alive in Christ and saved by Him, through and because of the atonement.

"Speaking of the Prophet's statement that all children are saved in the celestial kingdom, President Joseph Fielding Smith said: 'This would mean the children of every race. All the spirits that come to this world come from the presence of God and, therefore, must have been in His kingdom . . . Every spirit of man was innocent in the beginning; and all we that rebelled were cast out; therefore, all who remained are entitled to the blessings of the gospel.' *(Doctrines of Salvation,* 2:55.)

How and why are they saved?

"They are saved through the atonement and because they are free from sin. They come from God in purity; no sin or taint attaches to them in this life; and they return in purity to their maker. Accountable persons must become pure through repentance and baptism and obedience. Those who are not accountable for sins never fall spiritually and need not be redeemed from a spiritual fall which they never experienced. Hence, the expression that little children are alive in Christ. 'Little children are redeemed from the foundation of the world through mine Only Begotten,' the Lord says. *(D&C 29:46.)*

Will they have eternal life?

"Eternal life is life in the highest heaven of the celestial world; it is exaltation; it is the name of the kind of life God lives. It consists of a continuation of the family unit in eternity. We have quoted scriptures saying that children will be saved in the celestial kingdom, but now face the further query as to whether this includes the greatest of all the gifts of God—the gift of eternal life. And in the providences of Him who is infinitely wise, the answer is in the affirmative. Salvation means eternal life; the two terms are synonymous; they mean exactly the same thing. Joseph Smith said, 'Salvation consists in the glory, authority, majesty, power and dominion which Jehovah possesses and in nothing else.' *Lectures on Faith, pp. 63-67.)* We have come to speak of this salvation as exaltation—which it is—but all of the scriptures in all of the standard works call it salvation. I know of only three passages in all our scriptures which use salvation to mean something other and less than exaltation.

"Abinadi said, 'Little children also have eternal life.' *(Mosiah 15:25.)* Joseph Smith taught, 'Children will be enthroned in the presence of God and the Lamb; . . . they will there enjoy the fullness of that light, glory, and intelligence, which is prepared in the celestial kingdom.' *(Teachings of the Prophet Joseph Smith, pg. 200.)* President Joseph Fielding Smith spoke very expressly on this point: 'The Lord will grant unto these children the privilege of all the sealing blessings which pertain to the exaltation. We were all mature spirits before we were born, and the bodies of little children will grow after the resurrection to the full stature of the spirit, and all the blessings will be theirs through their obedience, the same as if they had lived to maturity and received them on the earth. The Lord is just and will not deprive any person of a blessing, simply because he dies before that blessing can be received. It would be manifestly unfair to deprive a little child of the privilege of receiving all the blessings of exaltation in the world to come simply because it died in infancy . . . Children who die in childhood will not be deprived of any blessing. When they grow, after the resurrection, to the full maturity of the spirit, they will be entitled to all the blessings which they would have been entitled to had they been privileged to tarry here and receive them.' *(Doctrines of Salvation,* 2:54.)

Will children be married and live in the family unit?

"Certainly, there can be no question about this. If they gain salvation, which is eternal life, which is exaltation, it means that they are married and live in the family unit. President Joseph Fielding Smith has so stated in plain words, and it is something that must necessarily be so." (See *Doctrines of Salvation,* 52:49-57.)

Why do some children die and others live?

Are those who die better off than those who remain in mortality?

"We may rest assured that all things are controlled and governed by Him whose spirit children we are. He knows the end from the beginning, and He provides for each of us the testings and trials which He knows we need. President Joseph Fielding Smith once told me that we must assume that the Lord knows beforehand who shall be taken in infancy and who shall remain on earth to undergo whatever tests are needed in their cases. This accords with Joseph Smith's statement: 'The Lord takes many away, even in infancy, that they may escape the envy of man, and the sorrows and evils of this present world; they are too pure, too lovely, to live on earth.' *(Teachings, pp. 196-97.)* It is implicit in the whole scheme of things that those of us who have arrived at the years of accountability need the tests and trials to which we are subject and that our problem is to overcome the world and attain that spotless and pure state which little children already possess.

How much do children know before their mortal birth about God and the plan of salvation?

"Every person born into the world comes from the presence of God. We all saw Him in that eternal world. We heard His voice. He taught us His laws. We learned about Christ and chose to follow Him when He was chosen to be our Savior and Redeemer. We understood and knew the gospel plan and shouted for joy at the privilege of getting our mortal bodies as part of that great plan of salvation. Returning pure and spotless to their Maker, children—who in reality are adults—will again have that gospel knowledge which once was theirs.

Will children ever be tested?

"Absolutely not! Any idea that they will be tested in paradise or during the millennium or after the millennium is pure fantasy. Why would a resurrected being, who has already come forth from the grave with a celestial body and whose salvation is guaranteed, be tested? Would the Lord test someone who cannot fail the test and whose exaltation is guaranteed? For that matter, all those billions of people who will be born during the millennium, when Satan is bound, 'shall grow up without sin unto salvation' *(D&C 45:58)* and therefore will not be tested. 'Satan cannot tempt little children in this life, nor in the spirit world, nor after their resurrection. Little children who die before reaching the years of accountability will not be tempted.' *(Doctrines of Salvation, 2:45-57.)* Such is the emphatic language of President Joseph Fielding Smith.

What is the age of accountability?

"Accountability does not burst full-bloom upon a child at any given moment in his life. Children become accountable gradually, over a number of years. Becoming accountable is a process, not a goal to be attained when a specified number of years, days, and hours have elapsed. In our revelation the Lord says, 'They cannot sin, for power is not given unto Satan to tempt little children, until they begin to become accountable before me.' (D&C 29:47.) There comes a time, however, when accountability is real and actual and sin is attributed in the lives of those who develop normally. It is eight years of age, the age of baptism. (D&C 68:27.)

"This principle of accountability has been twisted and perverted and even lost at various times. It was at the root of Mormon's inquiry to the Lord about infant baptism. (See Moro. 8.) One of our most instructive passages on the point contains the words spoken by the Lord to Abraham. 'My people have gone astray from My precepts, and have not kept Mine ordinances, which I gave unto their fathers,' the Lord said.

'But have turned from the commandment, and taken unto themselves the washing of children, and the blood of sprinkling.' (Gen. 17:4-6, Inspired Version.)

"Infant baptism was practiced by some even in those early days. The reason? Men no longer understood the atonement. For, as the record continues, those ancient peoples 'said that the blood of the righteous Abel was shed for sins; and have not known wherein they are accountable before me.' (Gen. 17:7, Inspired Version.)

"Then the Lord made this promise to Abraham: 'I will establish a covenant with thee, and it shall be My covenant between Me and thee, and thy seed after thee, in their generations; that thou mayest know for ever that children are not accountable before Me until they are eight years old.' *(Gen. 17:11, Inspired Version.)*

What about the mentally deficient?

"It is with them as it is with little children. They never arrive at the years of accountability, and are considered as though they were little children. If because of some physical deficiency, or for some other reason unknown to us, they never mature in the spiritual and moral sense, then they never become accountable for sins. They need no baptism; they are alive in Christ; and they will receive, inherit, and possess in eternity on the same basis as do all children.

"After revealing that little children are redeemed from the foundation of the world through the atoning sacrifice of Him who died to save us all, and after specifying that Satan has no power to tempt little children until they begin to become accountable, the Lord applied the same principles to those who are mentally deficient: 'And, again, I say unto you, that whoso having knowledge, have I not commanded to repent? And he that hath no understanding, it remaineth in Me to do according as it is written.' *(D&C 29:49-50.)*

When and with what stature will children be resurrected?

"Because they will receive a celestial inheritance, they will come forth in the first resurrection. President Joseph F. Smith said: 'Joseph Smith taught the doctrine that the infant child that was laid away in death would come up in the resurrection as a child; and, pointing to the mother of a lifeless child, he said to her: "You will have the joy, the pleasure, and satisfaction of nurturing this child after its resurrection, until it reaches the full stature of its spirit." There is restitution, there is growth, there is development, after the resurrection from death. I love this truth. It speaks volumes of happiness, of joy and gratitude to my soul. Thank the Lord He has revealed these principles to us.' *(Gospel Doctrine,* pgs. 455-56.)

What is our responsibility to our children?

"Lo, children are heritage of the Lord: and the fruit of the womb is His reward." *Ps. 127:3).* "Our children are our Father's children. He has entrusted them to us for a time and a season. Our appointment is to bring them up in light and truth so they will qualify to return to His Eternal Presence.

"Parents in Zion have a special responsibility for the care and well-being of the souls entrusted to them. King Benjamin summarized it in these words: 'Ye will not suffer your children that they go hungry, or naked; neither will ye suffer that they transgress the laws of God, and fight and quarrel one with another, and serve the devil, who is the master of sin, or who is the evil spirit which hath been spoken of by our fathers, he being an enemy to all righteousness.

'But ye will teach them to walk in the ways of truth and soberness; ye will teach them to love one another, and to serve one another.' *(Mosiah 4:14-15; see also D&C 68:25-28.)*

What, then, of this glorious doctrine concerning the salvation of children?

"Truly it is one of the sweetest and most soul-satisfying doctrines of the gospel! It is also one of the great evidences of the divine mission of the Prophet Joseph Smith. In his day the fiery evangelists of Christendom were thundering from their pulpits that the road to hell is paved with the skulls of infants because careless parents had neglected to have their offspring baptized. Joseph Smith's statements, as recorded in the *Book of Mormon* and latter-day revelation came as a refreshing breeze of pure truth: Little children shall be saved. Thanks be to God for the revelations of His mind where these innocent and pure souls are concerned!" (Bruce R. McConkie, *Passage to Light*, 1979, pgs. 75-87.)

Chapter Thirteen

Spirits, Cupids and Angels

M any people are reluctant to place even a small amount of trust in what Betty Eadie says, when on page 92 of the book *Embraced by the Light* she makes a reference to a young "male spirit" who was "playing cupid" with his future parents. Before we analyze this scenario to discover how devoid of truth it really is, let's look at who "Cupid" actually is.

Our Webster's Dictionary records: "Cupid—the Roman god of love, son of Venus, identified with the Greek god Eros. A representation of Cupid is a naked, winged boy with a bow and arrow."

It is interesting how Betty can find a place in her book supposedly about Jesus Christ, for pagan Roman and Greek gods of mythology. Ms. Eadie was not actually saying this "male spirit" was a Greek or Roman god; or that he was naked, winged and shot a bow and arrow. However, the image she expresses is just that in everyone's mind. Betty gives us the impression that angels look like this fictional mythological personage called "Cupid."

Let's read her exact words: ". . . I saw again the spirits who had not yet come to earth, and I saw some of them hovering over people in mortality. I saw one male spirit trying to get a mortal man and woman together on earth—his future parents. He was playing cupid and was having a very difficult time. The man and woman seemed to want to go in opposite directions and were unwittingly very uncooperative. This male spirit (cupid) was coaching them, speaking to them, trying to persuade them to get together. Other spirits became concerned as they saw his difficulty, and they took up the cause, several of them trying to 'corral' these two young people." *(Embraced by the Light,* pg. 92.)

Now, of course, this really didn't happen to Betty. She didn't really see this "little Cupid" angel or spirit flying around with wings and a bow and arrow, even though she implies as much. A great apostle of the Lord wrote some very revealing words regarding the false ideas that people have concerning heavenly angels. Elder George Q. Cannon said: "Joseph Smith had the necessary gifts and qualifications by which he was enabled to seek unto God with such irresistible faith that God heard his prayer and granted unto him the desire of his heart by revealing Himself unto him and giving unto him the instructions which He did. This was followed by other ministrations—the ministrations of angels. In the sectarian world you can scarcely see a picture of an angel without having a pair of wings attached, and every angel looks like a woman. Such ideas have come down through the ages. And who knew differently? Who could tell anything about it? As with the being of God Himself, so there were false conceptions concerning the character of angels, and there was no man who could correct them, because all were alike in ignorance, and all were alike a prey to the traditions that had been handed down. But when Joseph received the ministration of an angel—or angels, for he was visited by more than one—he saw that they were men, and that they had not feathered after death, that they did not have wings, but that they were glorified men, or men who had received glory from God; they were personages like they were on the earth. Thus a true conception began to dawn upon the minds of at least a few individuals, who believed Joseph's testimony concerning these beings. When I see our sisters and our brethren buying pictures of the sort to which I have alluded—pictures in which there are angels having wings—a sort of hermaphrodite beings, or worse—I wonder that they would hang such things on their walls, and then allow this false conception to be perpetuated in the minds of little children concerning the character of these heavenly beings. I think it is just as wrong to represent an idea falsely by a picture, as it is to teach it falsely by words, because an impression is made on the mind by either means. Pictures of that kind should not be patronized by our people. Our children should not be allowed to come to conclusions upon such false representations.

"How can men know anything about God, when He never speaks to them? How can men find out whether there is any revelation from heaven, when no revelation comes from that source? How can men find out about the future, if no one comes to tell them what the future is? It would be impossible for them to do it. It requires knowledge from God, concerning Himself; it requires knowledge concerning angels, it requires knowledge concerning eternity, to give men proper conceptions about these things. Hence it was that Joseph Smith, having had these visions opened to his mind, moved like a being from another sphere, among the children of men. God had opened his mind and revealed to him heavenly things. He saw them in their true light; he knew about them; and when he talked to men he was in their midst like a being from another world. That which he told them appeared, in some instances, to be false, to be nonsense. They could not comprehend it, because they had none of the Spirit of God about them, none of the knowledge of God, and they refused to accept him as an exponent of divine truth. So it is with the Elders who go out at the present day, to talk to the inhabitants of the earth. They are looked upon in the same light; though there is this to be said: that which has been taught by the Elders has had effect on the earth, and much misconception has gradually disappeared. *(Journal of Discourses 24:372-374.)*

"We ought to resist with all our might, mind, and our strength—influences which, if we would be led by them, would lead us to destruction—influences that are opposed to the Spirit of God—influences that would bring upon us destruction here and hereafter, if we would yield to them. These influences we have to resist. We have to resist the spirit of adultery, the spirit of whoredom, the spirit of drunkenness, the spirit of theft, and every other evil influence and spirit, that we may continually overcome; and, when we have finished our work on the earth, be prepared to govern and control those influences, and exercise power over them, in the presence of our Father and God. I have no doubt that many of my brethren and sisters have sensibly felt in various places and at various times evil influences around them. I have come to the conclusion that if our eyes were open to see the spirit world around us, we should feel differently on this subject than we do; we would not be so unguarded and careless, and so indifferent whether we had the spirit and power of God with us or not; but we would be continually watchful and prayerful to our Heavenly Father for His Holy Spirit and His holy angels to be around us to strengthen us to overcome every evil influence.

"When I see young men indulging in sinful practices, I come to the conclusion that they are led captive by the evil spirits around them. We call it the spirit of the evil one; but he has numerous agencies at work, even as the Lord has numerous agencies to assist him in bringing to pass the consummation of His great designs. The adversary has numerous agencies at his command, and he seeks to control and lead to destruction the inhabitants of the earth who will be subject to them. If we could see with our spiritual senses as we now see with our natural senses, we should be greatly shocked at the sight of the influences that prompt us to disobey the counsels of God or the Spirit of the Lord in our hearts. But we cannot see them, for they are spiritually discerned; and he who discerns the most, is the most fully impressed by the Spirit of God; he who does not discern, has not profited by the instructions given to him, and yields to those evil influences in an unguarded moment, and is taken captive in his blindness. He who is imbued with the Spirit of God is sensibly aware when the evil power approaches; but he does not welcome it to his bosom; he resists it with all the might and strength God has given unto him, and he obtains power over it, and it no more troubles him; if it does, its influence is more weakened than previously.

"We often talk about and desire to see angels. Every person who has joined this Church has had a desire to have revelations from God our Heavenly Father, and have knowledge poured out upon him as it was poured out in abundance upon the prophets of old. I merely suppose that this is so with everybody else, because I have these feelings myself, and judge others in this respect by myself. But, until we can learn to control and resist those evil influences that are now invisible, I think it would be unprofitable to have the administration of angels personally or visibly unto us. Until we can do this, I do not expect that we can have those other blessings profitably bestowed upon us. I do not expect that in the providence of God we will be favored with those other blessings until we can listen unto, and obey the counsels of, those appointed to preside over us. I know it is natural for people to be anxious to have some ministering spirit wait on them, and reveal itself unto them. For my own part, my reflections have caused me to view this in a different light than I viewed it in the beginning. I then thought it would be a great blessing to have that favor bestowed upon me. But when I have reflected upon the character and calling of the men whom God has called and sent in this generation—when I have thought of Brother Joseph Smith, and his greatness, his magnanimity, and his faith, I have thought, and still think, it is one of the greatest blessings of God upon me for Joseph to have been permitted to behold His face and to listen to His teachings. I feel the same now towards the present leaders of Israel. I am satisfied that this generation has been honored by as great prophets as ever stood before God upon the earth, excepting the Lord Jesus Christ; and how could I expect, if I disobeyed Brother Joseph Smith's counsel, that I could be favored with the presence and instruction of any being further advanced than he was when he was in the flesh? And so I feel in relation to Brother Brigham. He was one of the noblest sons of God, a man whom God endowed with the wisdom of eternity, with the power in part that is exercised in its fullness by the Gods of eternity. If we disobey his counsel, disregard his warning voice, and are careless respecting his teachings and the teachings of those associated with him, we are indeed unworthy of the presence of personages who have been glorified and who now dwell in the presence of God. I do not expect the day to come when this people will be favored with the administration of angels—with the presence of those holy and immortal beings—until we can learn to appreciate the teachings and instructions of the men of God in our midst. When that day does come that this people will implicitly obey the voice of those whom God has placed over them, and give heed to every instruction imparted to them by the spirit of revelation through the servants of God, then I shall expect visits from holy angels, and the glory and power of God to rest upon us to that extent it has never done hitherto; but I cannot well expect it before that time arrives, because if these blessings were to be bestowed upon us before we are prepared to receive them, I should fear they would turn to our condemnation, as they have done to many in the early history of the Church.

"There is nothing that we, as a people, have needed since our settlement in these valleys, and I may say since the organization of the Church, connected with the kingdom of God, in intelligence, in wisdom and counsel, that we have had to wait for. We have had line upon line, precept upon precept, here a little and there a little, from the beginning unto the present time, and there never was a day, an hour, a moment from the organization of this Church unto the present time that we, as a people, have been destitute of the voice of God and the instruction of the Holy Ghost. While this is the case, and we have abundance of teachings poured out upon us, and we should refuse to obey any of them, we need not expect visitations from higher personages, coming down to administer unto us and impart unto us things that we could know." (*Journal of Discourses* 11:30-31.)

Chapter Fourteen

The Attorney And The Drunk

T here is a strange scenario which Betty Eadie and Curtis Taylor weave beginning on page 98. The chapter is titled, "The Drunken Man." Betty claims that the "heavens were scrolled back" and that she as able to view the earth again. She says her "vision" allowed her to see "a man lying in a drunken stupor on the sidewalk near a building." Betty goes on to say that the "drunken bum was lying in his wallow." She said that the alcoholic's spirit was revealed to her and that she "saw a magnificent man, full of light. Love emanated from his being, and . . . he was greatly admired in the heavens." *(Embraced, pgs. 98-99.)* Drunks are pitied in heaven; not admired!

Curtis and Betty write that in the pre-existence, the drunk personally chose to come to earth as a bum to teach his pre-existent attorney friend how to be compassionate. We read, "The drunk had sacrificed his time on earth for the benefit of another." This is incredible. It is inconceivable that our Father in heaven would permit, authorize or predestine a precious spirit for such a ridiculous life mission. Barry Drage very knowledgeably pointed out the fallacy in this "Eadie-ite" teaching by asking the following two revealing questions. First, would God ever use an individual's probationary estate (earth life) in a negative, illegal or immoral way, just to teach others? Second, would Heavenly Father waste a man's one and only opportunity for celestial exaltation just to teach a point? Of course not! Anyone who would believe this doctrine of predestination is not familiar with the scriptures and the true gospel of Jesus Christ.

Another principle that Betty and Curtis fail to understand is the capitalistic form of economics. They asked on page 100: "Why couldn't the Lord just prompt the attorney to share his money with others?" This was one of Betty's thoughts and she admits she was puzzled and had no answer to the question, or even a hint of understanding. There are many attorneys who are wealthy because of their hard work, talents and abilities. There are also some attorneys who are poor. Betty makes an assumption that the drunk on the street was a homeless derelict. Maybe the drunk was a wealthy doctor or attorney with an alcohol or drug abuse problem. Maybe Betty's "make-believe" attorney was wealthy and a drunk himself.

Is Betty Eadie trying to tell us that the rich attorney does not share his wealth with others? Does the attorney have a family and relatives and friends he supports financially? Does Betty's "greedy" attorney employ paralegals, law clerks, secretaries, process servers, investigators, legal consultants and share his wealth with all of the families they support? Does this "selfish" attorney that Betty speaks so poorly of, buy printing, office supplies and equipment; vehicles, homes, clothing and also hire all of the many repair people that are a necessity when you own assets? Does the attorney pay massive tax revenues to support a myriad of government workers in the city, state and federal bureaucracies? We could go on and on with this real life situation. But the bottom line is that Betty's imaginary attorney SHARES and SUPPORTS vast numbers of different people in varying ways with his wealth . . . just as many other wealthy professionals do every day.

Betty and Curtis believe that it would be best for the "bad attorney" to simply give, or dole out, money to the homeless drunk. This is not true charity as the Lord teaches. Charity comes from the heart, not the pocketbook. A grave disservice is done when all you do is blindly dole out a little change or money to those truly in need of greater help. The attorney's financial donation would be better spent through tithes and church offerings which would be distributed to those who are truly in need and to those who will not squander the money on frivolous or unnecessary purchases. For the attorney to give money to the drunk, as Betty suggests, would permit the alcoholic to obtain more liquor and further ruin his life. Serious counseling and committed treatment is what the drunk needs, and then proper training in order to be self-sufficient and gainfully employed by someone like the attorney. This is true Christian charity . . . to help someone help themselves. Simply doling out money does far more damage than it ever does good, especially when the recipients do not know how to handle their finances.

Again, it is very important to remember that the wealthy and prosperous individuals are very important and essential for the economic well-being of our society. If you need a job, you don't apply to a homeless person . . . you seek out someone with the financial means and the where-with-all to pay your wages. This is a true life principle and another verification that Betty did not see or experience the "vision" of the attorney and the drunken man as she flagrantly claims. Note that even if Betty had witnessed this scene about the drunk, he was in his sorry and pitiful condition because of his own actions and behavior and not because of anything the attorney had done.

Next time you see a "bum" holding a sign that says, "WILL WORK FOR FOOD," stop and ask him if he would be willing to do some simple yardwork for a day at your home. I tried this five times and each time they refused my offer of work and food. They wanted a free-money handout and nothing more. The "beggars" earned far more money each day from free donations than they would earn at a job. The "tin cup" donations were from people who felt they were being charitable and were trying to dissuade some false sense of personal guilt. I sometimes offered to give them food, or take them to a fast food counter for a sandwich, but they refused the offer. I soon discovered that they were not hungry at all, but had other plans for my hard earned money.

Now that Betty Eadie has sold over $20,000,000.00 worth of *Embraced by the Light* books, I wonder if she will be as freely giving of her $20 million to the homeless derelicts as she expected her fantasy attorney to be?

To further compound their "erroneous revelations" and false teachings, Betty and Curtis try to tell us on page 67 of *Embraced by the Light* that "most of us had selected the illnesses we would suffer here in mortality, and that some people chose the illness that would end their lives. Now this might make a number of sick people feel better about their lot in life, but it is not true. Betty said, "Some people choose to die in ways that will help someone else." Then it gets even more far fetched. Taylor and Curtis claim that: "A person may have chosen to die, for example, by stepping into the street and being hit by a drunk driver. This seems terrible to us, but within the pure knowledge of God, his spirit knew that he was actually saving this driver more grief later. The driver may have been drunk again a week after and hit a group of teenagers, maiming them or causing greater pain and misery than was necessary, but he was prevented because he was spending time in jail for hitting the person who had already completed his purpose on earth. In the eternal perspective, unnecessary pain was spared for the young people, and a

growing experience may have begun for the driver."
(Embraced, pg. 68.) This is fallacious, Betty!

With all of this false information, it is high time that we learn what is right and true from the inspired minds of some of our greatest apostles and prophets.

Elder LeGrand Richards explained that: "One of the much-misunderstood teachings of the holy scriptures is the principle of predestination, as taught by Calvin, one of the early reformers. Had he understood the principle of preexistence, that we all lived in the spirit world before we were born here upon the earth, it would have enabled him to understand how men could be *foreordained*, called, and chosen before they were born to do certain work upon the earth without being predestined. He would also have understood how, because of the Lord's acquaintance with the spirits of all His children, He could know in advance what they would do under given circumstances and conditions, even as earthly parents may know largely how their own children will react to given experiences.

"But the holy scripture does not sustain the extreme stand taken by many of that thought: (1) that some are predestined to eternal life and that regardless of what they do, they will achieve it, while others are predestined to eternal damnation, and if so predestined, there is nothing they can do about it; (2) that every act of our lives is predetermined before we are born, and we cannot deviate therefrom; and (3) that whatever happens to us in life is the will of the Lord.

"Such a belief would hold the Lord responsible for all the wickedness, disobedience, and unrighteousness in the world. If man is without free agency and choice, then God, who created man, must have done the choosing, and hence He and not man is responsible for the life of man.

"The explanation usually given is that all men are born subjects of eternal damnation, but that by the principle of grace, those whom the Lord elects to predestine may obtain salvation—none others. This view is usually called 'fatalism.'

"Let us consider Paul's statements on this subject:

'But in a great house there are not only vessels of gold and of silver, but also of wood and of earth; and some to honour, and some to dishonour.

'If a man therefore purge himself from these, he shall be a vessel unto honour, sanctified, and meet for the master's use, and prepared unto every good work.' *(2 Timothy 2:20-21.)*

"From this statement of Paul's to Timothy, it is clear that no matter what may be one's handicaps or limitations in life, by purging himself he may become 'a vessel unto honour, sanctified, and meet for the master's use, and prepared unto every good work.'

"In Paul's discussion of Pharaoh, it may appear that the ruler had no free will but was raised up for a certain purpose, and that he was without choice:

'For the scripture saith unto Pharaoh, Even for this same purpose have I raised thee up, that I might shew my power in thee, and that my name might be declared throughout all the earth.

'Therefore hath he mercy on whom he will have mercy, and whom he will be hardeneth.' *(Romans 9:17-18. See also Exodus 9:16.)*

"To understand this statement of Paul, one must keep in mind the principle of preexistence of spirits—that the spirits of all men lived with God in the spirit world before they were born in the flesh, and that the Lord sent certain of the noble and great spirits at a particular time to do a certain work. To illustrate, let us consider the call of the prophet Jeremiah:

'Then the word of the Lord came unto me, saying,

'Before I formed thee in the belly I knew thee; and before thou camest forth out of the womb I sanctified thee, and ordained thee a prophet unto the nations.' *(Jeremiah 1:4-5.)*

"In like manner, the Lord knew Pharaoh before he was born, and understood his character and how he would respond to certain circumstance and situations. Thus, as indicated, the Lord raised him up for a special purpose so that He might show His power in him. But this did not force Pharaoh in any way to do the things he did, any more than a nation is forced to do what it does. Pharaoh took his time in making up his mind to free the children of Israel:

'And Moses and Aaron came in unto Pharaoh, and said unto him, Thus saith the Lord God of the Hebrews, How long wilt thou refuse to humble thyself before Me? Let My people go, that they may serve Me.' *(Exodus 10:3.)*

"Pharaoh was chosen by the Lord and sent into this world at his particular time because the Lord knew him and how he would meet the situation into which he was placed, but he still had the right to exercise his free will." (Richards, LeGrand. "*A Marvelous Work and a Wonder*," pgs. 340-341, 343, 345-46, 349-350, Deseret Book Co., 1976.)

"The gospel of salvation has thus been placed within reach of all our Father's children, and each is given the right to choose for himself, as expressed in the poet's words:

> Know this, that every soul is free
> To choose his life and what he'll be,
> For this eternal truth is given
> That God will force no man to heav'n.

He'll call, persuade, direct aright,
And bless with wisdom, love, and light,
In nameless ways be good and kind,
But never force the human mind.
Freedom and reason make us men;
Take these away, what are we then?
Mere animals, and just as well
The beasts may think of heav'n or hell.
(William C. Gregg, Hymns, no. 240.)

Elder James E. Talmage, one of the Twelve Apostles of The Church of Jesus Christ of Latter-day Saints said, "In an interview with Abraham, the Lord revealed many things ordinarily withheld from mortals. Concerning this the patriarch wrote: 'Now the Lord had shown unto me, Abraham, the intelligences that were organized before the world was; and among all these there were many of the noble and great ones; And God saw these souls that they were good, and He stood in the midst of them, and He said: These I will make my rulers; for He stood among those that were spirits, and He saw that they were good; and He said unto me: Abraham, thou art one of them; thou wast chosen before thou was born.' *(Abraham 3:22-23.)*

"This is one of the many scriptural proofs that the spirits of mankind existed prior to their earthly probation—a condition in which these intelligences lived and exercised their free agency before they assumed bodily tabernacles. Thus the natures, dispositions, and tendencies of men are known to the Father of their spirits, even before they are born into mortality. The word of the Lord came unto Jeremiah, telling him that before he was conceived in the flesh he had been ordained to be a prophet unto the nations.

"Evidence is abundant that Jesus Christ was chosen and ordained to be the Redeemer of the world, even in the beginning. We read of His foremost position amongst the sons of God in offering Himself as a sacrifice to carry into effect the will of the Father. He it was, 'Who verily was foreordained before the foundation of the world.' *(1 Peter 1:20.)*

"The doctrine of absolute predestination, resulting in a nullification of man's free agency, has been advocated with various modifications by different sects. Nevertheless, such teachings are wholly unjustified by both the letter and the spirit of sacred writ. God's foreknowledge concerning the natures and capacities of His children enables Him to see the end of their earthly career even from the first: 'Known unto God are all His works from the beginning of the world.' *(Acts 15:18.)*

"Many people have been led to regard this foreknowledge of God as a predestination whereby souls are designated for glory or condemnation even before their birth in the flesh, and irrespective of individual merit or demerit. This heretical doctrine seeks to rob Deity of mercy, justice, and love; it would make God appear capricious and selfish, directing and creating all things solely for His own glory, caring not for the suffering of His victims. How dreadful, how inconsistent is such an idea of God! It leads to the absurd conclusion that the mere knowledge of coming events must act as a determining influence in bringing about those occurrences. God's knowledge of spiritual and of human nature enables Him to conclude with certainty as to the actions of any of His children under given conditions; yet that knowledge is not of compelling force upon the creatures." (Talmage, James E., *Articles of Faith*, pgs. 189-191.)

In direct contradiction to the false doctrine of predestination, the boy prophet, Joseph Smith declared that "all mankind may be saved by obedience to the laws and ordinances of the gospel." He taught that, "To every man is given an inherent power to do right or to do wrong. In this he has his free agency. He may choose the right and obtain salvation, or he may choose evil and merit abomination; but one man is not predestinated to do evil and another to do good."

". . . whosoever will come may come and partake of the waters of life freely; and whosoever will not come the same is not compelled to come; but in the last day it shall be restored unto him according to his deeds." *(Alma 42:27.)*

The following information given to us by Elder Bruce R. McConkie, is especially applicable to Betty Eadie and Curtis Taylor. *(See Embraced, pg. 68.)* It should educate them and correct their misinterpreted and misguided ideas of the pre-existence. Elder McConkie says, *"Predestination* is a sectarian substitute for the true doctrine of *foreordination.* Just as Lucifer 'sought to destroy the agency of man' in pre-existence *(Moses 4:3),* so through his ministers here he has taught a doctrine, based on scriptural distortions, of salvation and damnation without choice on the part of the individual. Predestination is the false doctrine that from all eternity God has ordered whatever comes to pass, having especial and particular reference to the salvation or damnation of souls. Some souls, according to this false concept, are irrevocably chosen for salvation, others for damnation; and there is said to be nothing any individual can do to escape his predestined inheritance in heaven or in hell as the case may be.

"It is true that the words *predestinate* and *predestinated* are found in the King James translation of some of Paul's writings *(Rom. 8:29-30; Eph. 1:5, 11),* but Biblical revisions use the words *foreordain* and *foreordained*, which more accurately convey Paul's views. However, even as the King James Version renders the passages, there is no intimation of any compulsion or denial of free agency, for one of the dictionary definitions of foreordination is predestination, meaning the prior appointment (in pre-existence) of particular persons to perform designated labors or gain particular rewards." (McConkie, Bruce R., *Mormon Doctrine*, pgs. 588-589.)

"To carry forward His own purposes among men and nations, the Lord *foreordained* chosen spirit children in the pre-existence and assigned them to come to earth at particular times and places so that they might aid in furthering His divine will. These pre-existence appointments, made 'according to the foreknowledge of God the Father' *(1 Pet. 1:2)*, simply designated certain individuals to perform missions which the Lord in His wisdom knew they had the talents and capacities to do.

"The mightiest and greatest spirits were foreordained to stand as prophets and spiritual leaders, giving to the people such portion of the Lord's word as was designed for the day and age involved. Other spirits, such as those who laid the foundations of the American nation, were appointed beforehand to perform great works in political and governmental fields. In all this there is not the slightest hint of compulsion; persons foreordained to fill special missions in mortality are as abundantly endowed with free agency as are any other persons. By their foreordination the Lord merely gives them the opportunity to serve Him and His purposes if they will choose to measure up to the standard He knows they are capable of attaining.

"Speaking of foreordination to spiritual callings, the Prophet Joseph Smith said: 'Every man who has a calling to minister to the inhabitants to the world was ordained to that very purpose in the Grand Council of heaven before this world was. I suppose that I was ordained to this very office in that Grand Council.' *(Teachings,* pg. 365.)

"Jeremiah records a similar truth relative to his foreordination to be 'a prophet unto the nations' *(Jer. 1:5)*, and Moses taught that the whole host of spirits born in the linage of Jacob were before appointed to come through that chosen line. *(Deut. 32:7-8.)* It was because of their pre-existent training, election, and foreordination that Christ was able to say of certain chosen ones, 'My sheep hear My voice, and I know them, and they follow Me.' *(John 10:27.)*

"There is scriptural record of many other instances of specific foreordination. Christ himself, was before chosen to come to this life as the Son of God and Redeemer of the world *(Moses 4:1-4; Abr. 3:27; 1 Pet. 1:19-20)*, 'the Lamb slain from the foundation of the world.' *(Rev. 13:8.)* Mary, the mother of our Lord, was before named for her sacred mission *(1 Ne. 11:18-20; Mosiah 3:8; Isa. 7:14)*, and John the Baptist received a pre-mortal commission to prepare the way for the first coming of the Son of Man. *(1 Ne. 10:7-10; Isa. 40:3; Matt. 3:3.)* The Twelve who in their mortal life were destined to follow our Lord were seen in vision by Nephi nearly 600 years before the assigned day of their mortal missions." *(1 Ne. 11:29, 34-36.)* (McConkie, Bruce R., *Mormon Doctrine*, pgs. 290-291.)

Betty Eadie's attempt to "celestialize" her personal belief of a solution to the homeless problem is a fraud. To take a personal belief or idea and testify that it was revealed to you by the Lord Jesus in heaven when you were there visiting, as Betty claims, is a fraud. To claim that an experience happened which really did not is false testimony . . . and Betty and Curtis and the other "Eadie-ites" know they have no basis in fact for their phony testimony!

Betty's solution to the "homeless drunk" problem was to have the Lord "prompt" the rich to share their money equally with the poor. Ms Eadie's solution was not through the Lord's law of tithing . . . but by direct doles and handouts. Rush

Limbaugh clarifies this view in his most recent book titled, *See I Told You So* when he wrote about the homeless.

'It is utopian, and therefore unrealistic, to expect that every citizen will eat equally every day of the year. It is utopian to expect that every citizen will be provided the exact health care that citizens want every day of the year. It is utopian to believe that suffering of any kind can be eliminated through government intervention and action. As I have told you, there will always be poor people, however earnestly we try to eradicate poverty.

'Certainly, it's honorable to attempt to reduce hunger, suffering, and poverty. But it is not realistic to expect that every citizen can be provided the same amounts of good food, comfortable housing, and fine health care. That is what communism and socialism tried to accomplish. Instead of producing utopia, instead of narrowing the gap between the haves and have-nots, the bourgeoisie and proletariat, they created a more rigid class structure. The ruling class arrogates all the power and riches to itself, while the rest of the people remain servants of the state. Just look around the world. Examine the societies that have attempted to make life more prosperous for people by relying on centralized authorities. You won't find much prosperity, and you won't find anything remotely resembling an equitable distribution of resources.

'Equality of outcome or result is impossible because no two individuals are alike. We all have different abilities, talents, desires, ambitions, capabilities, and other characteristics. There is no way these differences can be equalized—even by force. Today, in the name of fairness and equality, the U.S. government is coercing greater and greater amounts of wealth transfers and redistribution. The utopians believe it is unfair that some have so much and others have so little. They see themselves as glorified Robin Hoods.

'Once again, it doesn't work. If you penalize achievement
and punish success, there is less wealth produced for everyone.
This is the fatal flaw of utopianism. Also, the value to someone
of something that is given to him is always less than the value
of something he earned with his own blood, sweat, and tears.
This is the lesson that countless socialist governments have
learned in just the last five years." (Limbaugh, Rush Hudson
III. *See I Told You So*, Pocket Books/Simon & Schuster. New
York, NY, 1993. pgs 266-267.)

Chapter Fifteen

Prayers Are Not Laser Beams

C laiming a revelation from God, Betty Eadie says, "The heavens scrolled back again, and I saw the sphere of earth rotating in space. I saw many lights shooting up from the earth like beacons. Some were very broad and charged into heaven like broad laser beams. Others resembled the illumination of small pen lights, and some were mere sparks. I was told that these beams were the prayers of people on earth." *(Embraced by the Light,* pg. 103.)

With great scriptural insight, Jerry Lund depicts the fallacy in Betty's "new age" prayer philosophy and wrote: "In her (Betty's) chapter on prayer, the author says she had always believed that you had to "nag the Lord" (p. 105) in order to get a prayer answered. But she learned while in the spirit world that it is "never necessary to repeat requests unremittingly, as though He couldn't understand" (p. 107.)

"In the New Testament, there are two parables that teach just the opposite. The Parable of the Unjust Judge *(Luke 18:1-6)* teaches us that we are to "pray and not faint [an old English word meaning to give up]. *(Luke 18:1.)* The Parable of the Friend at Midnight *(Luke 11:5-9)* teaches a similar lesson."

Speaking of these parables, Elder James E. Talmage said:

"The Lord's lesson was, that if man, with all his selfishness and disinclination to give, will nevertheless grant what his neighbor with proper purpose asks and <u>continues to ask</u> in spite of objection and temporary refusal, with assured certainty will God grant <u>what is persistently asked</u> in faith and with righteous intent. No parallelism lies between man's selfish refusal and God's wise and beneficent waiting. There must be a consciousness of real need for prayer, and real trust in God, to make prayer effective; and <u>in mercy the Father sometimes delays the granting that the asking may be more fervent</u>" *(Jesus the Christ*, pg. 435, emphasis added.)

Prayers are not laser beams or sparks as Betty and Curtis would have us believe. Prayers are not seen; they are heard. An excellent description of how prayers are heard and answered is the experience which occurred to the great Prophet Elijah. To refresh your memory, the wicked queen Jezebel (after learning that Elijah had called down fire from heaven and consumed the alter and that her 450 prophets of Baal had been executed) sought Elijah in order to have him killed. An angel fed and guided Elijah to the mountain of the Lord called Horeb where Elijah camped in the cave. This occurred at the end of a grueling 40 days and 40 nights of fasting. *(See 1 Kings, chapter 18 and 19.)* Elijah and the scriptures instruct us in a very important element of the gospel and in the essential principle of prayer. It says in 1 Kings 19:12-13, "And after the earthquake a fire; but the Lord was not in the fire: and after the fire <u>a still small voice</u> . . . saying, What doest thou here, Elijah?" God spoke to the Prophet Elijah not with the voice of a strong wind like a hurricane, or an earthquake or a fire . . . but with "a still small voice." This is how prayers are heard and answered. Still small voices, silently emanating from the earnest minds and sincere hearts of true believers in Christ. This is what prayers are made of.

Betty Eadie and Curtis Taylor continue to twist the true gospel principle and practice of prayer. For example, on page 103, Betty said she "saw angels rushing to answer the prayers . . . they literally flew from person to person, from prayer to prayer . . . and were especially joyful when somebody prayed with enough intensity and faith to be answered immediately. They (the angels) always responded to the brighter, larger prayers first. I did notice, however, that insincere prayers of repetition have little if any light; and having no power, many of them are not heard." *(Embraced,* pgs. 103-104.)

Again, prayers are not sources of light that differ in intensity. Betty goes on to say that she "was distinctly told that all prayers of desire are heard and answered . . . and the beams project straight from us and are immediately visible." There is no basis in Christian scripture or in prophetic revelations which would constitute a belief that angels hear and answer prayers! This is heresy. We are to pray to God the Eternal Father in the name of Jesus Christ; and to no other! We do not pray to saints and we do not pray to angels. We do not pray to the virgin mother Mary; nor do we pray to a mother in heaven. We pray to our Father in Heaven and to Him only.

To further understand the principle of prayer, let's review what the Bible Dictionary so eloquently says:

"As soon as we learn the true relationship in which we stand toward God (namely, God is our Father, and we are His children), then at once prayer becomes natural and instinctive on our part *(Matt. 7:7-11.)* Many of the so-called difficulties about prayer arise from forgetting this relationship. Prayer is the act by which the will of the Father and the will of the child are brought into correspondence with each other. The object of prayer is not to change the will of God, but to secure for ourselves and for others blessings that God is already willing to grant, but that are made conditional on our asking for them. Blessings require some work or effort on our part before we can obtain them. Prayer is a form of work, and is an appointed means for obtaining the highest of all blessings.

There are many passages in the New Testament that teach the duty of prayer (e.g., *Matt. 7:7; 26:41; Luke 18:1; 21:36; Eph. 6:18; Philip. 4:6; Col. 4:2; 1 Thes. 5:17, 25; 1 Tim. 2:1, 8).* Christians are taught to pray in Christ's name *(John 14:13-14; 15:7, 16; 16:23-24.)* We pray in Christ's name when our mind is the mind of Christ, and our wishes the wishes of Christ—when His words abide in us *(John 15:7.)* We than ask for things it is possible for God to grant. Many prayers remain unanswered because they are not in Christ's name at all; they in no way represent His mind, but spring out of the selfishness of man's heart.

Book of Mormon references on prayer include *1 Ne. 18:3; Alma 34:17-28; Ether 2:14.*

Mrs. Eadie and Mr. Taylor falsely printed in the last line on page 106 of the "Embraced" book that: "He (God) answers all prayers perfectly." As we just finished reading in the Bible Dictionary and in the many scripture references noted earlier, all prayers are not answered!

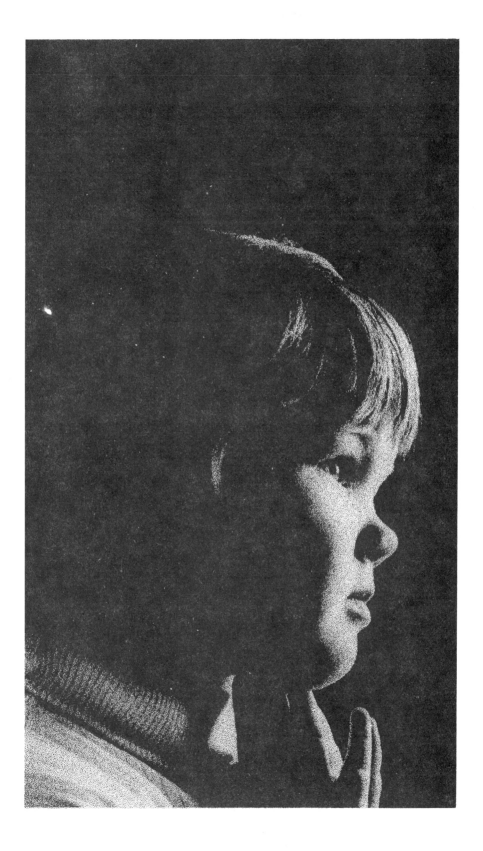

Chapter Sixteen

Betty's Tantrum Before Christ

I t is hard to believe that the authors of the fictional portrayal of Ms. Eadie's "flying tour" of the hereafter can feel honest about taking the gospel of Jesus Christ and twisting and changing it. When Eadie and Taylor can mold the doctrines of Christ to fit their own agenda, and take credit for the ideas, while at the same time claiming that the Savior revealed it to Betty is most astonishing!

Upon turning the pages of Betty's *Embraced by the Light*, you will see at the bottom of page 97 that Eadie claims personal ownership of this idea; "Then the thought came to me, referring to us all: 'If you could see yourself before you were born, you would be amazed at your intelligence and glory. Birth is a sleep and a forgetting.'" Betty's original thought just happens to have been written ages ago by the famous and renowned poet, William Wordsworth (1770-1850). He coined the often used phrase, "Our birth is but a sleep and a forgetting." With the reading of each page of the "Embraced" book, it becomes more and more difficult to believe anything Betty says. Betty Eadie and Curtis Taylor claim that Betty stood before a council of 12 men and was interviewed by them and by the Savior. After being firmly told that she must return to the earth because her mission was not complete, Betty boasts that she, "was not going back. I had learned as a child how to win a fight, and now I employed all those skills. I threw myself down and began crying. 'I won't go back,' I wailed, 'and nobody is going to make me! I'm staying right here where I belong. I'm through with earth!'" she screamed. *(Embraced,* pgs. 117-118.)

Can you imagine that? For an adult woman to throw a temper tantrum, by yelling, wailing, crying and throwing herself down would have been a spectacle to behold! Such childish and immature behavior at the feet of the Savior is appalling at best. Betty thinks her tantrums are skills. But since this experience didn't really happen except in Betty's comatose mind, it shouldn't matter. What is so serious is that Eadie and Curtis long for us to believe that it really did happen. A sheer fabrication!

Betty further embellishes this falsehood by stating that she extracted, "a promise from each person (Council of Twelve) present, including Jesus. I made them promise that the moment my mission (?) was complete they would take me back home. I was not willing to spend a minute on earth longer than was necessary. My home was with them. They agreed to my terms . . . ." *(Embraced, pgs. 118-119.)* What nerve to believe you could coerce and make deals with the Savior and other noble and elect spirits of God. Suppose Betty proves herself unworthy to return to the presence of God and "the twelve." Will they still be bound by their promise to Betty to let her "come back home" to them? Of course not. It does not take a great deal of intelligence or a spiritual confirmation to realize that this is just another of Betty's fictitious tales.

Should you happen to read the top of page 129 in the chapter entitled, "My Return," Betty says, "my spirit traveled in and out of both worlds, as if my return had not been permanent." Did Betty travel through the "tunnel" of death towards the bright light each time she died? How many times did Betty Eadie die . . . and then return? It is just too fantastic to even be believable.

Look at the bottom of page 139 of the "Embraced" booklet and you will read Betty claiming that she "was awakened by a messenger who stood by my bed. I understood that he had come from the spirit world. He said that the situation with my baby was not right, that she would be returned to me. He said that I would receive a phone call in which the caller would say, 'I have good news, and I have bad news.'" Now really, Betty; are we all expected to believe that heavenly messengers appear at the foot of your bed (as they did to the Prophet Joseph) to give you telephone messages? Totally unbelievable!

Elder Boyd K. Packer, speaking of personal revelation, gave the following counsel:

"I have learned that strong, impressive spiritual experiences do not come to us very frequently. And when they do, they are generally for our own edification, instruction, or correction. Unless we are called by proper authority to do so, they do not position us to counsel or to correct others. I have come to believe also that it is not wise to continually talk of unusual spiritual experiences. They are to be guarded with care and shared only when the Spirit itself prompts you to use them to the blessing of others" (*The Candle of the Lord, Ensign,* January, 1983, pg. 53.)

President Joseph Fielding Smith said:

"When a revelation comes for the guidance of this people, you may be sure that it will not be presented in some mysterious manner contrary to the order of the Church. It will go forth in such form that the people will understand that it comes from those who are in authority, for it will be sent either to the presidents of stakes and the bishops of wards over the signatures of the presiding authorities, or it will be published in some of the regular papers or magazines under the control and direction of the Church, or it will be presented before such a gathering as this at a general conference. It will not spring up in some distant part of the Church and be in the hands of some obscure individual without authority, and thus be circulated among the Latter-day Saints." *(Doctrines of Salvation* 1:287, emphasis in original.)

Betty is an "obscure individual, without authority." You come to the understanding and knowledge that what Betty Eadie claims as truth, is in fact, nothing more than a fanciful, well-organized plan to sell millions of books; it is much more fulfilling to read what a true prophet of God said . . . and for which he gave his very life as a witness. Please read the following testimony and pray about its truthfulness.

Joseph Smith stated that on September 21, 1823, he was visited by an angel sent from God. The angel said that Joseph was to be an instrument in bringing about the translation of an ancient book of scripture. The angel appeared to Joseph five times during the evening of September 21 and day of September 22, during which visits he detailed the mission of this young man. Joseph was seventeen at the time, and in the words dictated by him at a later date, he recalls vividly the visit of the angel:

"On the evening of the above-mentioned twenty-first of September, after I had retired to my bed for the night, I betook myself to prayer and supplication to Almighty God for forgiveness of all my sins and follies, and also for manifestation to me, that I might know of my state and standing before him, for I had full confidence in obtaining a divine manifestation as I previously had one. While I was thus in the act of calling upon God, I discovered a light appearing in the room which continued to increase until the room was lighter than at noonday, when immediately, a personage appeared at my bedside standing in the air for his feet did not touch the foot. He had on a loose robe of most exquisite whiteness. It was a whiteness beyond anything earthly I had ever seen; nor do I believe that any earthly thing could be made to appear so exceedingly white and brilliant. His hands were naked and his arms also a little above the wrists. So also were his feet naked as were his legs a little above the ankles. His head and neck were also bare. I could discover that he had no other clothing on but this robe as it was open so that I could see into his bosom. Not only was his robe exceedingly white but his whole person was glorious beyond description. And his countenance truly like lightning. The room was exceedingly light, but not so very bright as immediately around his person. When I first looked upon him I was afraid, but the fear soon left me. He called me by name and said unto me that he was a messenger sent from the presence of God to me and that his name was Moroni." *(Taken from a microfilm of the original manuscript found in the Church Historian's Office, The Church of Jesus Christ of Latter-day Saints, Salt Lake City, Utah.)*

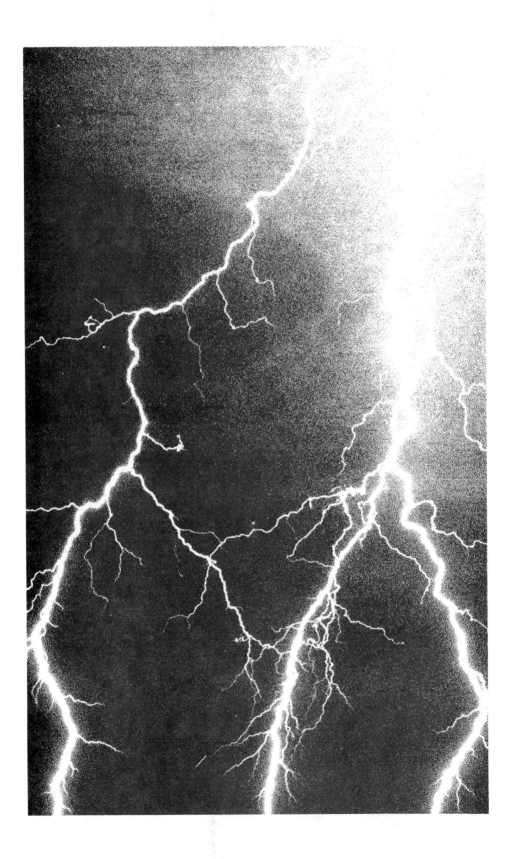

Chapter Seventeen

What Is An Evil Spirit?

"**I** was about to close my eyes and drift off to sleep when I caught a movement by the door. I tried to raise up on an elbow to get a better look, and I saw a creature poke its head in (the room). I cringed backward in fear. Then another (creature) appeared. They were creatures of the most hideous and grotesque appearance imaginable. Five of them entered the doorway, and I was all but paralyzed with fear. They appeared to be half-human half-animal—short, muscular beings with long claws or fingernails and savage, though human, faces. They came toward me, snarling, growling, and hissing. They were full of hate, and I knew that they intended to kill me. I tried to scream but was either too weak or too paralyzed with fear to move. I was helpless as they came to within five or six feet of the bed." *(Embraced,* pg. 126.)

The above quote from Betty is incredulous. It sounds more like a Stephen King novel, or a Steven Spielberg movie. This fictional illusion gets even better. Let's read on. Betty says, "Suddenly a huge dome of light, almost like glass, fell over me, and the creatures lunged forward, seeming to recognize its threat to them. The dome protected me as they frantically flailed at it and tried to climb on it to get a better vantage point. But the dome was too high to climb on, and they became more frustrated. They shrieked and cursed and hissed and began spitting. I was horrified as I felt trapped in my bed. The creatures were persistent, and I didn't know if the dome would hold up."

"When I thought I could bear it no more and my fear seemed about to overwhelm me, my three adoring angels, the monks, entered the room again, and the creatures fled. The angels said not to fear, that I was protected. They told me that the devil was angry at my decision to return to earth and that he had sent these powerful demons to destroy me. They said that the demons might try to get me again and that I might see or hear them in the future, but the dome would protect me. The demons came again after the angels left, but the dome kept them from me. I reached for the phone and called my husband and began to explain that there were demons in my room. He (Joe) thought I was hallucinating . . . and he hurriedly drove to the hospital. He could not see the creatures in the room . . . and . . . soon the creatures became frustrated and left again." (Embraced, pgs. 126-128.)

Now enough is enough. The imagination of Curtis and Betty when they drafted this fictional horror tale is incredible. The reason your husband Joe thought you were hallucinating again was because you WERE obviously hallucinating. The simple reason that Joe could not see the demons in the hospital room when you were all there within a few feet of each other was that there were no demons in the room. How did these 5 monsters get into the hospital and into your room without anyone else seeing them? What was this glass dome and how did it get into the hospital? How do the rest of God's children get a "lighted, protective glass dome" to protect us from "horrid monsters" sent by the devil to kill us?

It must be understood that the devil, or satan, once was an angel of light. Lucifer was made in the image of God our Father, just as each one of us was created in God's image. The devil is not crimson red. He does not have a tail with a spearhead at the end. He does not have horns protruding from his head, or cloven hoofs for feet, or sharp, jagged teeth. There is no fire shooting from his mouth or nose; no claws on his hands, no pointed ears and no wings!

The Bible Dictionary educates us about the devil, and explains that: "The English word devil, in the King James Version (of the Bible) is used to represent several different words in Greek, i.e., slanderer, demon, and adversary, and Hebrew, i.e., spoiler. The devil is the enemy of righteousness and of those who seek to do the will of God. Literally a spirit son of God, he was at one time an angel in authority in the presence of God; however, he rebelled in the premortal life, at which time he persuaded a third of the spirit children of the Father to rebel with him, in opposition to the plan of salvation championed by Jehovah (Jesus Christ). "Thus came the devil and his angels *(D&C 29:37.)* They were cast out of heaven, and were denied the experience of mortal bodies and earth life *(Isa. 14:12-13; Rev. 14:4-9; 2 Ne. 2:17; 9:8; D&C 29:36-38; 76:2-26; 93:25; Moses 4:1-4; Abr. 3:27-28.)*

"Latter-day revelation confirms the biblical teaching that the devil is a reality and that he does strive to lead men and women from the work of God. One of the major techniques of the devil is to cause human beings to think they are following God's ways, when in reality they are deceived by the devil to follow other paths.

"Since the devil and his premortal angels have no physical body of flesh and bones, they often seek to possess the bodies of mortal beings. There are many such instances recorded in scripture *(Matt. 9:32; 12:22; Mark 1:24; 5:7; Luke 8:30; Acts 19:15; Mosiah 3:6.)* Such can be evicted by the power of faith in Jesus Christ and the exercise of the holy priesthood. Jesus gave this power to His disciples *(Matt. 10:1; Mark 16:17; Luke 10:17; Acts 5:16; D&C 84:67.)*

"He (the devil) is miserable in his situation, and 'stirreth up the children of men unto secret combinations of murder and all manner of secret works of darkness.' *(2 Nephi 9:9.)* Satan tries to imitate the work of God by transforming himself nigh unto an angel of light *(2 Cor. 11:12-15; D&C 128:20.)* The devil is also a worker of miracles, by which he deceives many upon the whole world (Rev. 12:19.) In fact, the scripture says he deceives many upon the earth. Satan can cite scripture to make his point seem plausible. All of this is his scheme to make man miserable like himself. Protection against the influence of the devil is found by obedience to the commandments and laws of the gospel of Jesus Christ. The message of all the prophets and apostles is that truth, righteousness, and peace shall in the end prevail over error, sin and war; the faithful shall triumph over all their afflictions and enemies, and shall triumph over the devil. There shall be a complete and lasting victory of righteousness over wickedness on this earth, which will be done by the power of the Lord." *(KJV Bible Dictionary,* pgs. 656-657.)

The scriptures are replete with references explaining that the devil and his dark-angel demons are spirits made in the likeness and form of God, just as all men are. Satan and his demons are not half-animal monsters with long claws and hideous, grotesque creatures as Betty described. Quite the contrary. Many of the most devilish and satanic spirits on the earth are some of the most handsome and outwardly beautiful people you have ever seen. We must not let ourselves be fooled by pleasing looks and tempting visions of loveliness. Pornography and sexually oriented materials and broadcasts are prime examples of how Lucifer can package and display his superhighway to hell.

There are no lighted, glass bubbles or domes which are placed over you for protection against the devil as Betty claims. Your "dome" of protection is your faith and belief in Jesus Christ and your constant ability to pray always and be believing. We read in 3 Nephi 18:15, the words of the Lord when He said, "Verily, verily, I say unto you, ye must watch and pray always, lest ye be tempted by the devil, and be led away captive by him." The Apostle James, the brother of Jesus instructed you to: "Submit yourselves therefore to God. Resist the devil, and he will flee from you." *(James 4:7.)*

Again, it is important to remember that the devil's evil spirits can possess the bodies of human beings and have also been known to inhabit and possess the bodies of animals or swine as Luke records in chapter 8, verses 30 through 33. Evil spirits cannot inhabit half-animal, half-human bodies as Betty claims because there is no such thing as a half-human, half-animal on the face of the earth. If there is no such creature, how could a demon spirit inhabit such an imperceptible monster creation of Betty Eadie's. Impossible. It is quite possible that Betty was hallucinating or experiencing a nightmare, but a hallucinatory dream is not reality. As a self confessed hypnotherapist, maybe Betty was in a self induced hypnotic trance. Whatever it was, it was not a pack of creatures trying to kill Betty. It is not within the realm or power of demon angels to have the ability to physically kill or to "destroy" Betty as her three monks explained. *(Embraced,* pgs. 126-127.)

Betty and her writer Curtis Taylor stated on page 127 of the *Embraced by the Light* book that Betty's three "monk angels" told her that the "powerful demons" were there to destroy her because, "They told me that the devil was angry at Betty for returning to earth?" Betty's existence on earth is exactly where Satan wants her to be! With Betty here in mortality, she is still susceptible to the wiles and temptations of Lucifer and his demonic spirits. According to the devil's plan, he wants as much time as possible to turn every person against God. Once a person dies, Satan's ability to tempt that person dies also.

Chapter Eighteen

Embarrassed By The Fallacies

When you open the Webster's Dictionary and turn the pages to the definition of "fallacy," this is what you read: "aptness to mislead; a false or mistaken idea, opinion, etc.; error; false reasoning; illogical or misleading argument." This is an exact description, in every way, of Betty Eadie's and Curtis Taylor's book titled, *Embraced by the Light*. There are so many false, mistaken and dangerously misleading statements which these two novelists have conjured up, that it is difficult to address and expose them all.

For example, on page 63 of the "Embraced" book, Betty said that, "A body without a spirit cannot be healed; it cannot live for long." All Christians know that a body without a spirit is dead! Quoting James 2:26, "For as the body without the spirit is dead, so faith without works is dead also." A soul or spirit cannot live in a physically dead body; nor can a physical body continue to live once the spirit soul has departed!

On page 83 of "Embraced," Betty speculates that: "If our deaths are traumatic, the spirit quickly leaves the body, sometimes even before death occurs. If a person is in an accident or fire, for example, their spirit may be taken from their body before they experience much pain. The body may actually appear still alive for some moments, but the spirit will have already left to be in a state of peace." Well this sounds very nice, but it doesn't work that way. This false idea is just another of Betty's fantasies. There are millions of examples worldwide where people have suffered greatly at the time of death. Many individuals suffer agonizing deaths from burns or disease, and linger on and on for many days, weeks, months and even years! We must thank our Father in heaven that when He designed and constructed our marvelous physical bodies, He built into the brain and nervous system various means of coping with pain and often alleviating and blocking misery and acute suffering. Miracle drugs and medications are also available to help reduce some of the suffering of the seriously ill.

Should you read further on, you discover Betty and Curtis telling us (page 84) that, "Some who die as atheists, or those who have bonded to the world through greed, bodily appetites, or other earthly commitments find it difficult to move on, and they become earth-bound." Our Savior, as He was suffering crucifixion and hanging on the cross told the thief dying next to Him, "Today shalt thou be with me in paradise." (Luke 23:43.) All who die enter into the spirit world; some to spirit paradise and many others to spirit prison where they are taught gospel principles. Spirits are not earth-bound!

Betty and Curtis must have a dismal view of the great importance of our physical bodies. On page 123 of Embraced by the Light, Betty says, "I stood in the air and looked down at it (her body) and was filled with revulsion. It looked cold and heavy and reminded me of an old pair of coveralls that had been dragged through mud and grime . . . I had to put that heavy, cold, muddy garment on. If I thought about it one second longer I would lose my courage and flee . . . The body's cumbersome weight and coldness were abhorrent . . . I had become a prisoner of the flesh again." *(Embraced, pgs. 123-124.)* The human body is sacred and holy in nature. The Lord calls it a "temple" when He said, "Know ye not that ye are the temple of God, and that the spirit of God dwelleth in you? If any man defile the temple of God, him shall God destroy; for the temple of God is holy, which temple ye are." *(1 Cor. 3:16-17; 6:19; 2 Cor. 6:16; D&C 93:35; Alma 7:21; 34:36, Helaman 4:24.)* To regard the body, as Betty does, as an "abhorrent" dirty covering of flesh is to seriously minimize the importance God places upon our greatest earthly possession. To regard the human body as distastefully as Betty and Curtis do, is to minimize the damage we can do to our bodies through improper habits and abuses. It voids the importance of keeping our bodies clean and fit, and it ruins the incentive to prepare for a celestial resurrection. The Word of Wisdom and sexual purity seem less important when you accept the view of the body that Eadie and Taylor preach.

As a Bishop and an instructor in the Church Educational System, Jerry Lund reminds us that: "The Lord revealed to Joseph Smith that only when the elements (our physical bodies) are inseparably connected with our spirits do we have a fullness of joy *(D&C 93:33-35.)* We are told specifically that spirits view the separation from their physical bodies as a loss, not a blessing. Christ told the Twelve who lived with him during His ministry that they would look upon the long absence of their spirits from their bodies as a <u>bondage</u>" *(D&C 45:17.)* When Christ visited the spirit world after the crucifixion, even the righteous saints eagerly awaited "their redemption from the bands of death" and their "deliverance from the chains of death" so their bodies and spirits could be "united never again to be divided, that they might receive a fullness of joy" *(D&C 138:16-18.)*

It is still very baffling why Betty and Curtis refused to admit and proclaim their true church affiliation. A strong belief in Christ would mandate that a "Christian soldier" stand up and be proud, and shout from the highest mountain top that they were baptized and endowed members of The Church of Jesus Christ of Latter-day Saints (Mormon). Are they embarrassed . . . *Embarrassed by the Light*? On page 76 of their book *Embraced by the Light* they wrote that Betty "understood that all things of importance are created spiritually first and physically second. I had no idea of this before." As a Christian, and a Mormon, Betty must have read Moses 3:4, 5, 7 which reads in part: ". . . I, the Lord God, made the heaven and the earth, And every plant of the field before it was in the earth, and every herb of the field before it grew. For I, the Lord God, created all things, of which I have spoken, spiritually, before they were naturally upon the face of the earth . . . nevertheless, all things were before created; but spiritually were they created and made according to my word."

Shouldn't credit and praise be given where it is due? How can Curtis Taylor and Betty J. Eadie continue to take portions of the gospel of Christ and twist it to their own liking and to fit it to their own wishful thinking and then purposely withhold the source of origin. Even the word "paradisiacal" *(Embraced, pg. 122)* which refers to the new heaven and the new earth during and after the millennium, is solely a Mormon doctrinal term, not found in any secular dictionary, nor is it used in any other church, other than in The Church of Jesus Christ of Latter-day Saints. Again, why do Betty and Curtis have such an aversion to admitting their current association with the Mormons? There is no honest or reasonable justification to hide. Their *Embarrassed by the Light* of truth which is now shining upon them both.

Another good example of an eternal truth which Betty claims as her own, but is only found in Mormonism, is when she refers incorrectly to "the light of Christ" on page 91 and again on page 92. Betty talks about "allowing the light of

Christ to enter our lives." The light of Christ is given to every person born upon the earth. The Bible Dictionary says: "The phrase "light of Christ" does not appear in the Bible, although the principles that apply to it are frequently mentioned therein. The precise phrase is found in Alma 28:14, Moroni 7:18 and D&C 88:7. Biblical phrases that are sometimes synonymous to the term "light of Christ" are "spirit of the Lord" and "light of life" (see for example, *John 1:4; 8:12.*) The "spirit of the Lord," however, sometimes is used with reference to the Holy Ghost, and so must not be taken in every case as having reference to the light of Christ.

"The light of Christ is just what the words imply: enlightenment, knowledge, and an uplifting, ennobling, persevering influence that comes upon mankind because of Jesus Christ. For instance, Christ is 'the true light that lighteth every man that cometh into the world.' *(D&C 93:2; John 1:9.)* The light of Christ fills the 'immensity of space' and is the means by which Christ is able to be 'in all things, and is through all things, and is round about all things.' It 'giveth life to all things' and is 'the law by which all things are governed.' It is also 'the light that quickeneth' man's understanding *(see D&C 88:6-13, 41.)* In this manner, the light of Christ is related to man's conscience and tells him right from wrong *(cf. Moro. 7:12-19.)*

"The light of Christ should not be confused with the personage of the Holy Ghost, for the light of Christ is not a personage at all. Its influence is preliminary to and preparatory to one's receiving the Holy Ghost. The light of Christ will lead the honest soul who 'hearkeneth to the voice' to find the true gospel and the true Church and thereby receive the Holy Ghost." *(see D&C 84:46-48.* Additional references are *Alma 19:6; 26:3; D&C 20:27.)*

Betty has a propensity to fabricate, prevaricate and exaggerate. For example, during a nationally televised interview broadcast on "SIGHTINGS" (hosted by Tim White) Mrs. Eadie said, "I was able to ask thousands, even millions of questions and all were answered."

Now if Betty asked the Lord a question and received His answer, and it took no longer than one minute for this exchange, it would take Betty two years (694 days or 99 weeks) to process one million questions. Betty testified that she asked "millions" of questions on her visit with Jesus. If Betty were telling the truth, but of course she isn't, it would have taken her over four years to complete all of her questions—that's if she quizzed the "heavenly beings" continually, non-stop, day and night! Betty said she was dead only 4 hours.

This is nothing but a hoax by Betty Eadie. She will probably try to explain away this blatant falsehood by saying that the questions and answers were "non-verbal" and took place at the "speed of light," and lasted only milliseconds instead of many years as would normally be required. This would drastically exceed the speed with which the Lord conversed with His prophets. God speaks to all of His prophets and apostles "as one man speaketh to another" in order for His leaders here upon the earth to fully and completely understand what they are being told.

If Betty Eadie were telling the truth, and our Father in heaven did answer "millions" of questions for Betty, then she would be a million times more knowledgeable regarding spiritual matters than all of God's prophets and apostles combined! This is ludicrous! Why would the Lord reveal a million times more information to Betty J. Eadie than He would to His chosen and worthy leaders?

Why would Heavenly Father speak "with the speed of light" to Betty when it took four lengthy visits by the Angel Moroni to instruct the Prophet Joseph Smith? Each of the four visits of the ancient Prophet Moroni (appearing as a glorified, perfected angel of God) were exactly the same, and took place "without the least variation" except for slight cautions and enhancements at the conclusion. The four simultaneous and identical visions were needed to "clearly, distinctly and deeply impress upon Joseph's mind" in order that the *Book of Mormon* instructions would never be forgotten! *(see JS-H 1:30-49. Pearl of Great Price.)*

Why would the Lord answer millions of questions for Betty Eadie and then erase the questions and answers from her mind? For what purpose did this occur? Why did she wait almost two decades to tell us of her amazing journey through the universe and her other "tall tales?" Was God trying to send His people a message through Betty Eadie? Of course not! The fifth Article of Faith of The Church of Jesus Christ of Latter-day Saints reads: "We believe that a man must be called of God, by prophecy, and by the laying on of hands by those who are in authority, to preach the Gospel and administer in the ordinances thereof."

Betty Eadie's life, and for that matter, everyone's life will be much happier and full of joy if they will just tell the truth. William J. "Bill" Bennett is quoted as saying in his wonderful compilation titled, *The Book of Virtues* on page 599 that: "To be honest is to be real, genuine, authentic, and bona fide. To be dishonest is to be partly feigned, forged, fake, or fictitious. Honesty expresses both self-respect and respect for others. Dishonesty fully respects neither oneself nor others. Dishonesty fully respects neither oneself nor others. Honesty imbues lives with openness, reliability, and candor; it expresses a disposition to live in the light. Dishonesty seeks shade, cover, or concealment. It is a disposition to live partly in the dark."

(Bennett, William John. *The Book of Virtues* published by Simon & Schuster, New York, NY, 1993. pg. 599.)

This book, *Embarrassed by the Light* does just what Bill Bennett suggests in the paragraph above. It "shines the light of truth" on the many false and perverse ideas which Betty Eadie and the "Eadie-ites" proclaim and testify of. It forces the writers and contributors of Betty's book, *Embraced by the Light*, to come out of the dark into the light and be open about their many errors and fabrications.

In Betty Eadie's attempt to know all of the secrets of the universe and all of God's ways and the unrevealed nature of the heavens beyond, she has been tricked by the Adversary into proclaiming falsehoods as truth. Read carefully what Elder Dallin H. Oaks of the Quorum of the Twelve Apostles wrote about our desire to know everything. Elder Oaks said,

"Another strength Satan can exploit is a strong desire to understand everything about every principle of the gospel. How could that possibly work to our detriment? Experience teaches that if this desire is not disciplined, it can cause some to pursue their searchings beyond the fringes of orthodoxy, seeking answers to obscure mysteries rather than seeking a firmer understanding and a better practice of the basic principles of the gospel.

"Some seek answers to questions God has not chosen to answer. Others receive answers—or think they receive answers—in ways that are contrary to the order of the Church. For such researchers, Satan stands ready to mislead through sophistry or spurious revelation. Persons who hunger after a full understanding of all things must discipline their questions and their methods, or they can approach apostasy without ever knowing it. It may be just as dangerous to exceed orthodoxy as it is to fall short of it. The safety and happiness we are promised lie in keeping the commandments, not in discounting or multiplying them." (Oaks, Dallin H. *"Our Strengths Can Become Our Downfall." The Ensign.* October 1994. pg. 13.)

The popularity of Betty Eadie's and Curtis Taylor's book, *Embraced By the Light,* has been phenomenal because of the vast numbers of "lost souls" looking for answers to life's most important questions. These precious individuals must not be led astray with inaccurate teachings and false revelations, regardless of how popular Betty's book has become.

Elder Dallin Oaks proceeds further by teaching us in the same *Ensign* magazine article (pg. 15) cited above that:

"Another illustration of a strength that can become our downfall concerns charismatic teachers. With a trained mind and a skillful manner of presentation, teachers can become unusually popular and effective in teaching. But Satan will try to use that strength to corrupt teachers by encouraging them to gather a following of disciples. A Church teacher, Church Education System instructor, or Latter-day Saint university professor who gathers such a following and does this 'for the sake of riches and honor' *(Alma 1:16)* is guilty of priestcraft. 'Priestcrafts are that men preach and set themselves up for a light unto the world, that they may get gain and praise of the world; but they seek not the welfare of Zion' *(2 Ne. 26:29.)*

"Teachers who are most popular, and therefore most effective, have a special susceptibility to priestcraft. If they are not careful, their strength can become their spiritual downfall. They can become like Almon Babbitt, with whom the Lord was not pleased, because "he aspireth to establish his counsel instead of the counsel which I have ordained, even that of the Presidency of my Church; and he setteth up a golden calf for the worship of my people" *(D&C 124:84.)*

May we all earnestly seek the truth by following the Lord's anointed and chosen leaders; His apostles and prophets administering in His church. The Church of Jesus Christ of Latter-day Saints and the fullness of the gospel of Jesus Christ found within the *Book of Mormon* are the means of passage and re-entry back into the kingdom of God. The knowledge that Christ lives and reveals His will to His prophet today will bring you the greatest peace, joy and happiness when you dedicate your life to living His gospel. You will then find yourself "standing in the bright light" as our Lord and Savior manifests the truthfulness of His gospel plan to you by the power of the Holy Ghost.

Use this handy order coupon to order additional copies of the
following books if your bookstore is sold out . . . .

How Many?	Name of Publication	Price Per Copy
_____	Embarrassed By the Light	$ 9.95
_____	All About Angels - Vol. 1	8.95
_____	All About Angels - Vol. 2	8.95
_____	The Miracle of Love	8.95
_____	About The Three Nephites	9.95
_____	Passage to Light	9.95
_____	The Missionary Kit	9.95
_____	The Carthage Tragedy	9.95

Please send me the book(s) listed above. I have enclosed a check or
money order for $_____ plus $1.95 for each book
ordered for postage, shipping, packaging, tax and delivery. Please allow
four weeks for your special delivery. You will receive a free gift book with
your order of five or more books. Cut out this order form and mail it to:

Mail Services — World Library
LDS BOOK PUBLICATIONS, INC.
P. O. Box 1515
Provo, Utah 84603-1515

Send Book(s) to:

_____
Name

_____
Mailing Address

_____
City   State   Zip

Use this handy order coupon to order additional copies of the following books if your bookstore is sold out . . . .

How Many?	Name of Publication	Price Per Copy
_____	Embarrassed By the Light	$ 9.95
_____	All About Angels - Vol. 1	8.95
_____	All About Angels - Vol. 2	8.95
_____	The Miracle of Love	8.95
_____	About The Three Nephites	9.95
_____	Passage to Light	9.95
_____	The Missionary Kit	9.95
_____	The Carthage Tragedy	9.95

Please send me the book(s) listed above. I have enclosed a check or money order for $_____ plus $1.95 for each book ordered for postage, shipping, packaging, tax and delivery. Please allow four weeks for your special delivery. You will receive a free gift book with your order of five or more books. Cut out this order form and mail it to:

Mail Services — World Library
LDS BOOK PUBLICATIONS, INC.
P. O. Box 1515
Provo, Utah 84603-1515

Send Book(s) to:

_____
Name

_____
Mailing Address

_____
City   State   Zip